CREATIVE THINKING AND PROBLEM SOLVING IN GIFTED EDUCATION

Third Edition

JOHN F. FELDHUSEN
Purdue University

DONALD J. TREFFINGER
State University College at Buffalo

Kendall/Hunt
Publishing Company
Dubuque, Iowa

Originally entitled: TEACHING CREATIVE THINKING AND PROBLEM
SOLVING

Library of Congress Catalog Card Number: 85–51523

ISBN 0–8403–3762–0

Printed in the United States of America
10 9 8 7 6 5 4 3 2

CONTENTS

LIST OF REVIEWS IN CHAPTER SIX

PREFACE

We were thrilled by the excellent reception to the earlier editions of this book. Hundreds of teachers in cities throughout the United States told us that they found the book to be a valuable guide in developing plans to teach creative thinking and problem solving. However, it is obvious to us that the book has been especially valuable to teachers in gifted education programs. Both of us have attended numerous workshops, conferences and conventions on gifted education, and it was chiefly in that context that we learned about the great need of teachers for such guidance in developing gifted education programs.

We were also pleased to learn that our reviews of instructional material were a valuable guide to school personnel seeking material for gifted education programs. We learned that many schools simply ordered all the materials we recommended.

Thus, this edition of our book focuses more directly on the gifted. There is an entire chapter on teaching creative thinking and problem solving to the gifted, creative and talented. Other chapters have been substantially revised, especially Chapter Four, "Methods of Teaching Creativity and Problem Solving." Our reviews of instructional material, as presented in Chapter Six, have also been greatly revised. Many new materials have been added. Some have been dropped.

We hope that this new edition of our book will help teachers do a better job of teaching creativity and problem solving to the gifted, creative and talented. These youth are our great hope for the future. Sound programs of gifted education will meet their special needs and help them bring their potential to fruition in the arts, professions, business, government, and sciences.

John F. Feldhusen
Donald J. Treffinger

Chapter 1

TEACHING STUDENTS TO THINK

The first purpose of this book is to help teachers teach students how to think and especially how to think creatively and solve problems. Much time in the classroom is spent teaching information and basic skills in reading, language arts, science, social studies, and mathematics. Very little is used to teach students how to use information and basic skills in thinking, solving problems, or creating new ideas.

A second purpose of this book is to help teachers learn how to teach creative thinking and problem solving to gifted, creative and talented children. Gifted children have high intellectual and academic ability. Creative children have the ability to develop new ideas. Talented children have special abilities in one area such as music, art or drama. All these gifted children need special help in developing their gifted potential.

Creative thinking is the ability to think of a lot of ideas where there is a problem or a need for ideas (Gallagher, 1975). It is also being able to think of many different ideas, to think of unique or original ideas, and to develop or elaborate ideas. Sometimes it is asking good questions which clarify a problem. It is also being able to translate ideas into forms of communication or expression which make it possible for other people to grasp the ideas or solution to problems. Thus, it is necessary to find words or use art media, music, drama, or movement to express our ideas, solutions, or feelings.

Problem solving is a complex set of skills and abilities. Guilford and his associates (Guilford and Hoepfner, 1971; Merrifield, Guilford, Christensen, and Frick, 1962) have carried out extensive research on problem-solving abilities. They conclude that there is no single problem-solving-ability. Instead, there are a number of abilities involved in the complete problem-solving process. They concluded from their factor analytic studies of problem solving that the following abilities are major cognitive functions in problem solving: (1) thinking rapidly of several characteristics of a given object or situation; (2) classifying objects or ideas; (3) perceiving relationships; (4) thinking of alternative outcomes; (5) listing characteristics of a goal; and (6) producing logical solutions (1971, pages 104–107).

We have combined creativity and problem solving into a single complex concept following the model proposed by Guilford and his associates. Many discrete creative abilities such as fluency, flexibility, and originality, while measureable and trainable separately, are in reality indispensable components of realistic and complex problem solving behavior. Puzzle type problems might involve only restricted logical thinking abilities. Real life problem solving is really creative problem solving in that it requires a wide range of creative, conceptual and logical thinking abilities.

It is a frequently expressed goal of American education, at all levels, to foster cognitive growth among children, and particularly to help children think creatively and to become better problem solvers.

In her text, *Growing Up Gifted,* Clark (1983) stated the case as follows:

> "Cognitive development rests on the analysis, integration, and evaluation of a vast quantity of experience of the environment and on an understanding of those experiences. Educational programs should provide for an array of experiences and for encouraging the processes of understanding, analyzing, organizing, integrating, and evaluating. Qualitatively different planning for the gifted implies recognition of the ways in which their differential cognitive characteristics affect these processes. (P. 195)

In his review of creativity theory and research Stein (1974) summarizes as follows:

> "Our knowledge may not be complete in all respects, but we do know a good deal about the motivational and personality characteristics of creative individuals as well as their cognitive characteristics—perception, thought processes, and problem-solving behavior. Consequently, it seems reasonable to assume that creativity can be stimulated if individuals are helped to become more like those persons who are known to be creative. (P. 7)

The importance of research on creativity and problem solving more specifically has been described by Parnes (1967), Torrance (1965, 1967), Torrance and Myers (1970), Guilford (1967) and others. Davis (1973) has also provided an excellent review and interpretation of problem solving and creativity research in his book *Psychology of Problem-Solving Theory and Practice* and in his more recent book (1981) *Creativity is Forever.* Callahan's book (1979) *Developing Creativity in the Gifted and Talented* also offers excellent supportive evidence for the importance of teaching creative thinking skills to the gifted, and it provides good guidelines for such teaching.

Clark also lists the different cognitive characteristics of the gifted which in turn give rise to special needs. These needs impose demands upon the teacher to alter teaching methodology for the gifted:

> "Extraordinary quantity of information; unusual retentiveness
> Advanced comprehension
> Unusually varied interests and curiosity
> High level of language development
> High level of verbal ability
> Unusual capacity for processing information
> Accelerated pace of thought processes
> Flexible thought processes
> Comprehensive synthesis

Early ability to delay closure
Heightened capacity for seeing unusual and diverse relationships
Ability to generate original ideas and solutions
Early differential patterns for thought processing (e.g., thinking in alternatives, abstract terms, sensing consequences, making generalizations)
Early ability to use and form conceptual frameworks
An evaluative approach to themselves and others
Persistent goal directed behavior" (P. 195)

In a recent comprehensive review on problem solving and inquiry as cognitive processes and the trainability of these thinking skills Glaser (1984) asserts that ". . . an effective strategy for instruction involves a kind of interrogation and confrontation. Expert teachers do this effectively, employing case method approaches, discovery methods, and various forms of Socratic inquiry dialogue (P. 101)." Glaser concludes his review with an optimistic statement of what we can achieve in teaching thinking skills:

"Psychological knowledge of learning and thinking has developed cumulatively through S-R formulations, Gestalt concepts, information-processing models, and current knowledge-based conceptions. With deepening study of cognition, current research and development is increasing the likelihood that we can move to a new level of application at which a wide spectrum of thinking skills is sharpened in the course of education and training. Few other educational possibilities beckon us to apply our energies and exploratory talents as much as this one. Teaching thinking has been a long-term aspiration, and now progress has occurred that brings it into reach. The cognitive skills developed by people in a society are profoundly influenced by the ways knowledge and literacy are taught and used. We should take heed. The task is to produce a changed environment for learning—an environment in which there is a new relationship between students and their subject matter, in which knowledge and skill become objects of interrogation, inquiry, and extrapolation. As individuals acquire knowledge, they also should be empowered to think and reason." (Pp. 102–103)

In an increasingly complex, ever changing, challenging and problem-ridden world, people of all ages have great need to be good creative thinkers and good problem solvers. However, the greatest hope for improving thinking lies with children in school. It is easier to arrange the conditions in school to help children learn how to think than to try to change adults, most of whom are no longer involved in formal education.

We attempted to assemble and evaluate a large amount of information about teaching materials and methods, especially for teaching creative thinking and problem solving. However, it was found that such materials are often closely related to the teaching topics of inquiry and critical thinking. Therefore, these topics are dealt with in reviews whenever some aspect of creativity or problem solving was identified as a part of critical thinking and inquiry.

It was also recognized very early in the preparation of this book that most of the time in typical classrooms is devoted to the usual curricular or subject matter areas such as social studies, language arts and reading, science and

3

mathematics. Thus, it was decided that it might be best to give teachers information on how to teach thinking within regular subjects as much as possible.

Finally, it was recognized that a lot of guidance and direction from teachers on the job would be needed. Thus, nearly one hundred teachers in Atlanta, Kansas City, Indianapolis, and Los Angeles were interviewed. In addition, questionnaires were given to hundreds of other teachers in grades kindergarten to six. Thus, a great deal was learned about teachers' needs, problems and concerns in trying to teach children how to think.

An Overview of This Book

Chapter 2 is concerned with the rationale of and goals for creative learning, with particular emphasis on their importance for gifted, creative and talented students. While creative thinking and problem solving skills are important and relevant for *all* learners, we believe that gifted, creative and talented students have special need for opportunities to develop and use them at a high level. Four models for effective programs for creative learning and enrichment are described.

Chapter 3 considers the implications of the four models for programs for gifted, creative, and talented students. In addition to general implications for planning or designing programs, specific attention will also be given to unique considerations at both the elementary and secondary levels.

Chapter 4 presents information about teaching methods or techniques which can be readily adapted by the teacher to fit any grade level and subject area. These are methods and techniques for teaching creative thinking, problem solving, and inquiry. Often no special materials are needed. No AV equipment is needed. However, it will usually be necessary to adapt the technique to fit a particular grade level or subject matter.

Chapter 5 provides more specific directions on how to get a project started in the classroom. It gives detailed directions for creativity and problem-solving exercises and procedures for implementing them in the classroom. Chapter 5 also presents guidelines for developing learning modules or packages for teaching creative thinking and problem solving.

Chapter 6 presents the descriptions of published *teaching material* for specific grade levels and subject areas. It is divided into two main sections. The first section includes reviews of commercially published materials dealing with creativity and problem solving. The second section includes reviews of books that can be used, either through the suggestions that they give on methods of teaching creative thinking or problem solving or by actually using them as stimulus materials. The best way to use this chapter is as a reference source to familiarize yourself with the great variety of materials that are available. In this way you will be better able to choose materials to fit your specific needs.

Many cities throughout the United States are organizing school programs for gifted, creative, and talented students. In some of these programs the regular classroom teacher is assisted by a resource teacher in developing activities in the classroom. In others, the students meet after school or Saturdays with a special resource teacher. Still others set up special classes for the gifted, creative, and talented. Whatever the administrative arrangement, the teachers must search for and develop materials and methods which will stimulate intellectual and creative growth in these students. The ideas presented in this book are intended to help these teachers in their work with gifted, creative, and talented students.

Summary

The first purpose of this book is to help teachers learn how to teach creative thinking and problem solving to gifted, creative and talented students. The second purpose of this book is to help teachers learn about promising materials, methods and techniques for teaching creative thinking and problem solving in their classrooms. In many schools teachers are developing broad new methods for open and individualized instruction. Most of the material reviewed and presented in this book for teaching creative thinking and problem solving will work well in open and individualized classrooms. Creative thinking and problem solving are intensely personal and individual experiences which thrive in an open classroom climate. However, teachers who maintain a more traditional classroom organization will also find that many of the materials and methods are adaptable to their needs and organization. A wealth of good ideas and good materials is available for teachers who are industrious, intelligent, creative, and motivated to apply them in their classrooms.

Chapter 2

TEACHING CREATIVE THINKING AND PROBLEM SOLVING TO THE GIFTED, CREATIVE AND TALENTED

Gifted, creative and talented students have several kinds of immediate and long range needs. Perhaps their major long range needs are to be able to realize their full career potential and to be able to experience a sense of personal fulfillment or self actualization in maturity. For students with the highest levels of potential, we expect careers that will result in high level creative productions, inventions, or solutions to major societal problems. The *immediate* needs of the gifted may be to have educational and personal experiences which will eventually facilitate their progress toward the long range goals, help them develop important skills, and yet provide immediate happiness and satisfaction.

What kinds of instructional activities serve those immediate needs of the gifted, creative and talented? We can readily identify nine different kinds of activities which can serve the needs of gifted, creative, and talented students in school. Some of these can also be served by parents and other agencies outside of the school, of course. These activities are:

1. maximum achievement of basic skills and conceptual understanding in school subjects
2. learning activities appropriate to the student's level of academic achievements
3. a large fund of information about diverse topics
4. exposure to a variety of potential fields of study and occupations
5. development of awareness and acceptance of their own capacities, interests, and needs
6. experience in creative thinking and problem solving
7. stimulation to pursue higher level goals and aspirations
8. development of independence and self-direction in learning
9. experience in relating effectively with other people

The first need is for maximum achievement of basic skills and conceptual understanding in school subjects. This need is closely linked to the second, learning activities appropriate to the student's level of academic achievement. The pace and depth of instruction in most classrooms is geared to a hypo-

7

thetical "average" student. Often there may be no opportunity for gifted students to pursue skills and concepts at the deeper level for which they have the ability. For gifted students who have managed to learn at an accelerated pace, this means engaging in classroom activities well below their appropriate achievement levels. Gifted students suffer particularly in this respect in mathematics and science. Often the door is open in language arts and social studies for the student to forge ahead even without help from the teacher. Sometimes the help comes from parents or outside agencies, sometimes simply from books and reading.

Individualized basic instruction, appropriate enrichment programs, and formal acceleration procedures can and should be developed for gifted students who are advanced achievers. Figure 2.1 suggests some approaches at the different grade levels. Teachers and school administrators are often reluctant to accept any forms of acceleration, but they are needed for gifted students who are highly advanced achievers (Kulik and Kulik, 1984).

The gifted also have great need to master basic skills in mathematics, science and language arts to facilitate their overall learning in school. Language arts skills are especially vital in all learning activities which involve reading and writing. Gifted students can do much to facilitate their own learning if they can master the basic skills and use them in further learning situations.

The third need of gifted students is for a large fund of information. Many gifted students are ardent seekers of information. They read encyclopedias, dictionaries, atlases, and fact books as well as general literature and become great storehouses of seemingly idle information. In truth such an information reservoir can be the base for much creative thinking. Creatively gifted students can call forth varied information to develop many possibilities, to form new associations, and to think of unusual ideas in solving problems. A large storehouse of information seems to be indispensable.

This need for a large fund of information can be met through a variety of experiences in interaction with people, through reading, and through opportunities to explore, try out, and experience directly. Teachers and parents need to provide abundant opportunities to gifted children for reading, for travel, for visits to historical and cultural sites, art experiences, and interactions with people. There should also be much emphasis on information transmission in any special classes or individualized work for the gifted.

The fourth need is for exposure to a variety of potential fields of study and occupations. These experiences should come quite early for gifted students. In part they constitute career education, and many schools are instituting such programs. However, gifted students' needs go well beyond conventional career education programs. They need much exposure to higher level occupations, art careers and biographies of creatively productive people to help them become aware of their own potential and possible goals to strive for.

8

For Whom?	(a)	Children who are at or above the 95% ile on standardized achievement tests for initial screening.
	(b)	Children who are two or more grade levels above grade placement on standardized achievement tests.
Primary Level Provision?	(a)	Individualized or small group activity to provide advanced instruction in math, science, language arts or social studies.
	(b)	Early admission to school.
	(c)	Grade advancement.
Upper Elementary?	(a)	Special accelerated groups for instruction in math, science, English and social studies.
	(b)	Early admission to higher level high school courses.
High School?	(a)	Special accelerated groups for instruction in math, science, English and social studies.
	(b)	Early admission to advanced high school courses.
	(c)	Organize college level courses to be offered in high school.
	(d)	Release students to take college courses in vicinity.
	(e)	Special summer programs of courses at college and universities.

Figure 2.1. Acceleration for very high achievers

Activities in this area are complementary to those in the fifth area, development of awareness and acceptance of their capacities, interests, and needs. Many gifted students fail to realize and understand their own abilities, aptitudes and achievements. This self knowledge is critically related to the exploration of careers and fields of study. Gifted students must come to see optimum links between their own abilities and potential careers.

The next area of instructional activities, the sixth, is creative thinking and problem solving. Gifted students need activities in this area to help them expand their capacity for high level invention, inquiry and discovery. Full use of abilities in achieving maximum potentials means that many gifted students will produce new, unique, original contributions in their fields as adults. Early experience in creative thinking and problem solving paves the way, helps the children learn how to use divergent thinking capacities and creative problem solving. They should also become aware of the potency of creative thinking and problem solving as "mental tools" to achieve new heights of invention and production.

In the seventh area, gifted students need stimulation to pursue higher level goals and aspirations commensurate with their potential. Teachers and parents can encourage them and successful adults can serve as models. Gifted students growing up in poverty or minority family situations may lack both encouragement and models. The school may have to become the principal source of those influences. Persistent and helpful mentors can help meet this need. Teachers can give much encouragement. In a sense this seventh need is for motivational stimulation commensurate with the gifted student's potential. Highly productive adults have often identified their goals very early in life and have been able to concentrate their efforts during the school years toward achievement of those goals. The motivational intensity and level must be extremely high for the gifted if they are to achieve their full potential.

The eighth goal addresses the need for gifted students to learn how to manage and direct their own learning, and to become effective in independent inquiry. In part, this involves learning how to use methodological and research skills and library or reference materials. But it also means learning at home and in school how to "take command" of their own learning. Parents and teachers should not expect gifted students to know how to do these things naturally or spontaneously. They must be taught how to set goals, identify and locate resources, formulate and carry out plans, and evaluate their work. Adults should also expect gifted students to develop these skills *gradually* (Treffinger & Barton, 1979).

Finally, the ninth goal deals with relating effectively with other people. We do not want to encourage the development of adults who are intellectual "giants" but socially or interpersonally inept. It is important for individuals to be able to function skillfully and happily with many other persons of varying ages, interests, and abilities.

The Important Role of Creativity in Enrichment Programs

In delineating the special needs of gifted, creative and talented students, we have explicitly suggested that experiences in creative thinking and problem solving are essential for gifted, creative and talented students because we want to pave the way for high level success in these skills in maturity. We assume that the necessary mix in maturity includes:

1. strong basic abilities
2. skill in creative thinking and problem solving
3. facilitative environmental conditions to foster high level creative production

We further assume that the experience in creative thinking and problem solving should begin early and be promoted both in school and in the home. The Goertzels (1978) have documented well the role of home and family relationships in the lives of eminent contributors to society.

This need to teach the skills of creative thinking and problem solving and to provide experience therein cuts across the entire range of a child's development from infancy (Starkweather, 1971) to adulthood (Parnes, Noller & Biondi, 1977). Thus, it obviously is not the kind of learning which can be neatly encapsulated in a semester or year of study. Rather, through a continuous program beginning in childhood we hope that basic skills and life styles which facilitate creative thinking and problem solving can be acquired, sustained, and strengthened.

In recent years, there has been increasing recognition of the important role of creativity in understanding the very *nature* of "giftedness." Gowan (1978, p. 9) argued, for example:

> At this point, it might be well to redefine giftedness as follows: *A gifted child is one who has the potential to become verbally creative; a talented child is one who has the potential to become non-verbally creative.* Such a definition emphasizes that giftedness is *potentiality* not *performance,* and gets us away from a definition using an arbitrary IQ cut-off score. [Italics in the original.]

Renzulli (1978) argued explicitly that creativity is a fundamental component of giftedness, and componential definitions of creative talent that are quite similar to Renzulli's "three rings" of ability, creativity, and task commitment have been described by Torrance (1979) and Amabile (1983). We believe, then, that there is considerable support for the position that creativity should be a fundamental consideration in our attempts to recognize and nurture the unique characteristics and learning needs associated with "giftedness."

Other reasons for us to consider creativity and problem solving to be important components of effective enrichment and instructional programming have been presented by Treffinger (1980) and Isaksen & Treffinger (1985). Creative learning and problem solving should be important to educators for several reasons; these include:

1. Creativity and problem solving help us to deal independently and effectively with many practical problems.
2. Creative learning and problem solving help us to cope with future problems and challenges that we may now be unable to anticipate. Effective learning can no longer be considered committing to memory all of the "right answers" that we will need, for we no longer are certain we *know* all the "right answers," or even the right questions!
3. The impact of creativity and problem solving on our lives can be very powerful. Most people remember, and feel very strongly and positively about, the experiences they have had with learning and solving problems in creative ways. Frequently such experiences can shape or direct the course of one's personal or professional life!
4. Involvement in creative learning and problem solving helps us to "balance" the creative and critical sides of our nature. We learn to be more effective in thinking, and more skillful in both generating and evaluating ideas, when we have learned to use the tools of creative learning and problem solving.
5. Even though creative learning and problem solving are not always easy, and may in fact be very difficult and demanding, most people find that productive involvement in them leads to great satisfaction and a sense of enjoyment or reward.

Thus, when you become a teacher who is concerned with creative learning and problem solving, the enrichment that will result for your students is indeed a very important part of successful education. We hear a great deal of talk these days about the importance of "excellence" in education. We believe that teaching that fosters creative thinking and effective problem solving contributes in very important ways to excellence.

It can, of course, be argued that these are appropriate activities for *all* children and should be taught to all children in regular classes. This argument is partly true but it neglects gifted students' needs for appropriately higher level, more abstract, and more challenging experiences in these activities. The levels of experience for the gifted might prove frustrating for average or *less* able youngsters. However, some teachers who conduct creative enrichment activities with the gifted in their classes report that less able youngsters can sometimes work effectively with gifted students in such project activity and that both, the gifted and the less able, profit from the experience.

Creative enrichment can also serve as a vehicle for attainment of other learning needs of the gifted as set forth earlier in this chapter, particularly the needs for:

1. maximum achievement of basic skills and conceptual understanding
2. exposure to fields of study and occupations
3. stimulation to pursue higher level goals

Ann Dirkes (1977) has shown that creative thinking techniques can be used to teach basic skills and concepts in mathematics. De Vito and Krockover (1980) presented models for use of creativity in science. Our own research (Feldhusen, Bahlke & Treffinger, 1969) indicated that through the teaching of creative thinking, children also made substantial gains in language skills.

Recent developmental work (Feldhusen & Kolloff, 1979; OrRico & Feldhusen, 1979) indicated that instruction in creative thinking and problem solving can be used to help gifted students learn about fields of study and higher level careers. The results of yet another project (Moore, Feldhusen & Owings, 1978) indicate that such career education activity stimulates gifted students to plan and strive for higher level educational and occupational goals.

Thus, we conclude that instruction in creative thinking and problem solving is fundamental in enrichment programs for the gifted. Some advocates of gifted programs argue that the sole and primary ingredient is acceleration. We have no quarrel with the need to accelerate instruction for the gifted, if that means something more than simply offering instruction earlier than usual. For the gifted acceleration ought to include larger amounts of information presented faster and earlier than the normal curriculum, increased abstraction in teaching, higher level verbal processing in reading and writing, and above all challenging instruction which stimulates the gifted to strive for mastery and understanding. In sum, acceleration should include early introduction to the tools of both convergent and divergent thinking as well as evaluation. One major purpose of this chapter has been to argue for the crucial role of divergent or creative thinking and problem solving in instruction for the gifted.

Models of Creative Learning and Enrichment

If creative learning and problem solving are essential components of an effective enrichment program, and are important aspects of effective instruction for gifted, creative, and talented students, what models can guide the educator's efforts? In this section, we will review briefly four models that we have found helpful in understanding creative learning and enrichment and which provide guidelines for instructional practice.

These models are: Feldhusen and Kolloff's (1978) Three Stage Model for Enrichment; Renzulli's (1977) Enrichment Triad Model; Treffinger's (1980) Creative Learning Model; and fourth, a general model emphasizing the use of Individual Educational Programs (Butterfield et al., 1979).

In each of these models, basic skills and strategies of creative thinking are presented as underlying "tools" or fundamentals to be learned as a prelude to the highest level of activity, independent project and problem solving activity. These models stress that there are some relatively discrete skills to be learned such as ideational fluency and elaboration in writing and design. Gifted children must especially have this underpinning to assure their later success in higher level creative activities. These basic level abilities also include mastery of drawing, writing, reading, and quantitative skills. Some of these can be acquired through the regular classroom activity and individualization of learning there. But others, especially those related to creative thinking, problem solving, and independent activity, are dealt with more effectively in special programming for the gifted.

The second level in these models calls for the provision of experience in broader strategies of creative thinking, problem solving, and project activity. One specific example involves application of the Creative Problem Solving model (Noller, 1977; Noller, Treffinger & Houseman, 1979; Parnes, Noller & Biondi, 1977). Synectics, morphological analysis, and research and inquiry strategies are all taught and experienced in this second stage. Creative enrichment models for the gifted all stress some form of these experiences as being fundamental parts of special programs.

The third stage of creative activity for the gifted calls for the highest level possible of creative, productive activity. Gifted, creative and talented students can work independently or in small groups at this level using basic skills and strategies acquired in stages one and two in addressing realistic complex problems. This is perhaps the ultimate strategy level. Teachers, parents, and/or mentors act as resource persons, guides, and stimulators, while the student(s) take(s) the initiative. One child may be writing about dinosaurs, while other children are writing a play which they will produce, writing a series of haiku poems, or studying rat reinforcement behaviors. Several students are also designing their own micro-computer. These are all appropriate stage three activities for gifted, creative and talented students.

The Three Stage Model

There was a time when enrichment for the gifted meant instruction carried out by the regular teacher for a gifted child in the regular classroom. Martinson (1972) concluded that such efforts to enrich instruction in the regular classroom were generally unsuccessful.

As described briefly earlier in this chapter, Feldhusen and Kolloff (1978) developed a creative enrichment model which stresses the development of basic

STAGE I	DEVELOPING BASIC DIVERGENT AND CONVERGENT THINKING SKILLS AND AFFECTIVE RESPONSES, TEACHER LEADS, SHORT TERM ACTIVITIES.
	EG. fluency, flexibility, originality, elaboration, logic, critical thinking, values clarification, self understanding
STAGE II	DEVELOPING HIGHER LEVEL COGNITIVE STRATEGIES, WORK-STUDY PRODUCTION SKILLS, STUDENTS TAKE MORE INITIATIVE.
	EG. creative problem solving, research methods, library skills, time management, interviewing, inquiry techniques, writing
STAGE III	DEVELOPING INDEPENDENCE IN RESEARCH AND CREATIVE PRODUCTION, STUDENTS TAKE INITIATIVE, TEACHER SERVICE AS RESOURCE PERSON AND GUIDE.
	EG. experimental research, writing reports, formal presentations, extended synthesis projects, creative performances

Figure 2.2. The Purdue three-stage model

thinking skills, cognitive strategies, and independent learning in gifted children. This model will be described next in greater detail (see Figure 2.2). Instruction in this model is supplementary to the regular curriculum and may include reading, language skill activity, mathematics, social studies, science and art, but all are proferred as supplements to the regular curriculum. The gifted students meet in small groups of six to twelve and pursue three kinds of activities (Feldhusen & Kolloff, 1978). It has also been adapted successfully to career education (OrRico & Feldhusen, 1979).

Stage one activities in the model are designed to teach and strengthen basic divergent, convergent, and imagination abilities and to foster basic language and mathematic skills. Activities at this level are selected and directed by the teacher. They are generally short term in nature requiring 15 to 30 minutes for a lesson. Good illustrations of divergent thinking and language arts skills are found in Renzulli and Callahan's *New Directions in Creativity* (1973). A fluency activity requires children to list things which are soft and blue. A language activity calls for antonyms and synonyms for given words. Excellent examples of convergent thinking skills are found in Harnadek's *Deductive Thinking Skills* (1978) and mathematics in Siegel and Wiseman's *Visual Thinking Skills for Reading and Math* (1978). Stage one activities can be seeded throughout the program. Information transmission via reading and listening is also a basic activity related to stage one. These activities are guided by specific objectives and are designed to foster basic skills and abilities in divergent and convergent thinking. Flack and Feldhusen (1983) presented a large number of future study activities which can be used to foster stage one skills. Gregory (1982) also presented guidelines and activities for fostering growth at stage one in art.

Stage two is concerned with fostering broader strategies using convergent, divergent, evaluative, and cognition skills. The gifted students assume somewhat more self direction in these activities, but the teacher is still basically the selector and director. There are many examples of this type of activity in Renzulli and Callahan's *New Directions in Creativity* (1973). Creating a new product, planning an advertising campaign, designing product packages, doing the layout for a space ship or writing a script are illustrations of this stage activities. Similarly teaching the creative problem solving model, synectics, morphological analysis, or logical analysis of arguments in a story are illustrations of these stage two strategies. The emphasis is on the teaching of broader and more practical cognitive skills and strategies. These activities are often longer in duration ranging from one to several hours and spreading over several days or weeks.

Stage three introduces gifted students to independent project activity in which they can use their basic skills and abilities, information acquired through reading and listening, and cognitive strategies taught in stage two to develop facility in self direction in larger and more realistic projects. The students explore their own experiential background and interests in defining projects. Motivation must be increasingly internal. Creativity is stressed. The teacher now assumes the resource role. The students plans and conduct their own investigation, inquiry, or project. The goal is to develop increased capacity for such self direction, self motivation and use of creative skills.

Stage three activities come to predominate in the model as children make progress in stage one and two. It is assumed that gifted children will spend two to six hours a week in some administrative arrangement for the three-stage program. The time working with a teacher might occur during the school day, after school or Saturdays. Feldhusen and Wyman-Robinson (1980) and Feldhusen and Sokol (1982) have described a Saturday program at Purdue University for gifted children in which the three-stage model is used in many different classes and a variety of subjects. Typically there is outside or home work carried on by the student when not in session with a teacher. The work or project activity may grow out of each of the basic curricular areas, mathematics, science, language arts and social studies. A sound program also offers continuing guidance in reading both in supplementary literature and in books related to project activity.

Who teaches this enrichment program? There are many alternatives. Some cost money, others do not. It is very helpful to have a paid special gifted resource teacher. Such a teacher can be trained intensively and can travel from school to school serving the programs in several locations. Resource teachers can also be hired part-time or combined with some other specialty such as a

16

coordinator in language arts. Other alternatives involve hiring unemployed teachers on an hourly basis, hiring parents who have college education, or recruiting others from the community who have expertise for the programs.

Feldhusen (in press) discussed the various approaches used in research on the teacher of the gifted. Early research focussed on the search for general characteristics of the good teacher of the gifted. Recent efforts have turned to the competencies which are essential and which can be taught in teacher training courses and workshops. Major competencies include skill in teaching creative thinking, problem solving, independent study, logic, inquiry, and critical thinking.

Some approaches to the application of this model require no special budget. In some schools the librarian meets with small gifted groups while an aide tends the library. Parent volunteers or community resource people can often be recruited without pay. Teacher volunteers may work with the gifted after school. Occasionally the teachers at a grade level organize themselves departmentally and free one of the team to work with the gifted a certain amount of time each week. Many alternatives are possible.

The program described here serves the needs of children who are moderately advanced in the basic curricular areas or creatively gifted. Those who are highly advanced in one or more areas should also be given some form of acceleration. Figure 2.1 shows various forms of acceleration which can be used across the K–12 spectrum. Achievement tests given as a part of the regular school testing program can be used to identify very high achievers (95% ile in math, or reading, or language skills). However, standardized achievement tests often fail to tap the true level of achievement of a gifted child because too low a form of the test is used in relation to grade placement. A gifted child in grade two taking a test for levels 1–3 would not have sufficient challenge to assess his/her highest potential level of performance. Children who are seen as possibly gifted should be tested with higher level forms of the test.

Research indicates (Getzels & Dillon, 1973) that acceleration is effective in improving achievement of gifted students. The major forms as shown in Figure 2.1 are early admission to school, grade advancement, special accelerated classes, college courses in high school, and early admission to college. All can be used successfully to accelerate educational programs for gifted children who are very high achievers in one or more areas of the curriculum.

Renzulli's Enrichment Triad Model

Another approach for describing enrichment for gifted and talented students is the *Enrichment Triad Model* (Renzulli, 1977; Renzulli & Smith, 1978). This model has also led its developer and his associates to formulate a flexible approach to identification and programming, known as the *Revolving Door Model,* in which the three levels of the Enrichment Triad play a central role (Renzulli, Reis, & Smith, 1981).

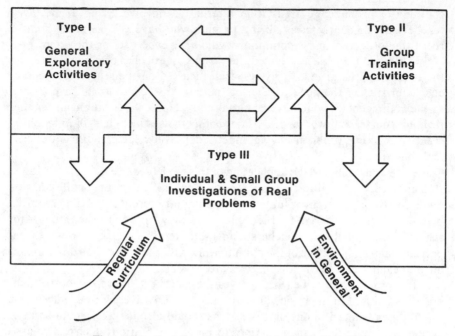

Figure 2.3. Enrichment Triad model (Renzulli, 1977)

The Enrichment Triad Model describes three levels of enrichment activities. Type I Enrichment, called "General Exploratory Activities," give students opportunities to "sample" a variety of topics outside the regular curriculum. Type II, called "Group Training Activities," provide opportunities for learning process, inquiry, and methodological skills. Type III, "Individual and Small Group Investigations of Real Problems," call for students to become "producers" of knowledge, not merely "consumers of other peoples' knowledge." Thus, Type III enrichment in this model places a strong emphasis on defining a real problem, formulating an original solution, developing a product, and sharing the results or products with appropriate audiences. The Enrichment Triad's three levels are illustrated in Figure 2.3.

Type I Enrichment may involve such activities as guest speakers, field trips, films or media presentations, or work with interest development centers in a classroom. Renzulli has stressed that many of these activities, and the content of many Type I enrichment efforts, is not only for a small percentage of students who have been designated as "gifted" on the basis of test scores. Indeed, some Type I Enrichment activities are clearly appropriate for *all* students. Others, such as lectures on technical subjects by "visiting experts," may neither appeal to nor be appropriate for all students, because of their greater level of abstractness and complexity. Type I Enrichment activities are an important component of enrichment programming, however, since they can help to clarify and focus the kinds of methodological and advanced content preparation the students will need to continue learning about a particular topic, and they can serve to "call attention" to many possible areas of study that can become the foundation for Type III investigations by students.

Type II Enrichment involves teaching students "process" skills, including methods of problem solving, thinking skills, research or inquiry methods of a general nature, and methods of research that are specific to disciplines in which students are particularly interested. In order to conduct Type III Enrichment projects successfully, students must be competent with the necessary research and inquiry tools or methods. Once again, some *general* methodological skills are undoubtedly necessary and appropriate for all students. Every student faces problems that must be solved, and can benefit from knowing specific methods and techniques to solve them more effectively. Most students will need to know methodological skills involving such topics as preparing a review of literature, using reference books, using the card catalog, and preparing footnotes and bibliographies. As gifted, creative, and talented students become involved in more complex investigations, however, it will also be necessary for them to learn and use much more complex and difficult methods, techniques, and resources.

Type III Enrichment, in Renzulli's model, is much more complex than the task of "going to the library and writing a paper about your topic" that has been so familiar to many generations of students under the name of "term papers" or "independent projects." Renzulli has emphasized that a true Type III investigation involves a problem for which the student has considerable motivation and emotional investment ("task commitment"), for which there is no known or pre-existing solution, and which will enable the investigator to contribute a new product or idea to the field of study (Renzulli, 1983, pp. 49–50). Students should not simply be "assigned topics" for Type III investigations, nor can they be expected to complete several such projects in a semester or year. Type III opportunities arise from the student's involvement and personal commitment to solving a particular problem in an effective and creative way.

The Enrichment Triad Model emphasizes the need for students to have a variety of exploratory experiences, and to learn to use many basic skills of critical and creative thinking, in preparation for interest-centered involvement in the investigation of real problems at a very high level of complexity and challenge.

Treffinger's Creative Learning Model

Treffinger (1980; Treffinger, Isaksen & Firestien, 1982, 1983) has also presented a model of creative learning that involves three levels or sequential stages. This model is illustrated in Figure 2.4.

19

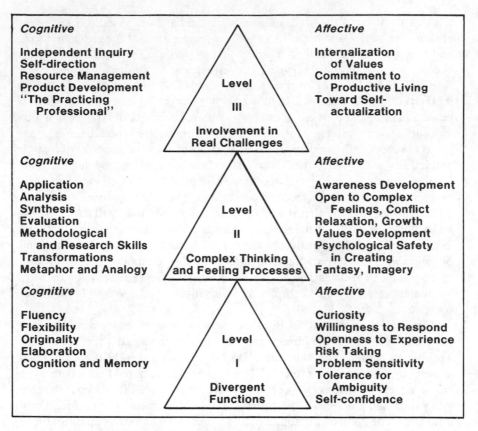

Cognitive		Affective
Independent Inquiry		Internalization
Self-direction		of Values
Resource Management	**Level**	Commitment to
Product Development		Productive Living
"The Practicing	**III**	Toward Self-
Professional"		actualization
	Involvement in	
	Real Challenges	

Cognitive		Affective
Application		Awareness Development
Analysis		Open to Complex
Synthesis	**Level**	Feelings, Conflict
Evaluation		Relaxation, Growth
Methodological	**II**	Values Development
and Research Skills		Psychological Safety
Transformations	Complex Thinking	in Creating
Metaphor and Analogy	and Feeling Processes	Fantasy, Imagery

Cognitive		Affective
Fluency		Curiosity
Flexibility		Willingness to Respond
Originality	**Level**	Openness to Experience
Elaboration		Risk Taking
Cognition and Memory	**I**	Problem Sensitivity
		Tolerance for
	Divergent	Ambiguity
	Functions	Self-confidence

Figure 2.4. Creative learning model. Treffinger, D. J. *Encouraging Creative Learning for the Gifted and Talented*. Ventura, CA: Ventura County Schools/LTI, 1980.

The model emphasizes that creative learning involves both a cognitive and affective dimension. Students' *thinking* and *feeling* processes must be considered as teachers plan ways to enrich their learning in creative ways.

The initial stage, or Level I, is called *Divergent Functions*. In this stage, students learn to use the basic "tools" that will enable them to work successfully with complex reasoning and problem-solving tasks at higher levels. Level I activities include many enjoyable and popular activities such as brainstorming, attribute listing, and SCAMPER. (These techniques will be described in greater detail in Chapter IV.) They can be easily related to many content or subject matter topics at a variety of grade levels.

Experiences with Level I activities are not sufficient for an effective enrichment program, however. They are not the ends in themselves, but rather they are *means* to the end of success in working with more complex challenges. Thus, it is important for the teacher to guide the students into Level II of the model, *Complex Thinking and Feeling Processes.* At this level, students learn and practice more complex methods and systems for creative thinking and problem solving. This can involve, for example, systematic work at various levels of Bloom's (1956) Taxonomy, participating in realistic (but not necessary "real") problems in such programs as Olympics of the Mind or Future Problem Solving, and practicing Creative Problem Solving with such group exercises as *CPS for Kids* (Eberle & Stanish, 1980) or *Be A Problem Solver* (Eberle & Stanish, 1984).

The ultimate purpose of instruction in creative learning, according to this model, however, is not that students should become proficient in *practicing* being thinkers or problem solvers with contrived (if interesting) problems of someone else's choosing, but rather that students develop confidence and competence in dealing with *real problems and challenges,* which is Level III. "Real" problems, as viewed in Treffinger's model, are those for which the student has a great deal of personal concern and involvement. In their description of "ownership" of a problem, Isaksen & Treffinger (1985) have emphasized three criteria: *interest* (whether you want to do something about the problem), *influence* (whether it is possible for you to take action on the problem), and *imagination* (whether you are really searching for new or creative solutions).

Treffinger's Creative Learning Model emphasizes the need for gradual or systematic development of creative thinking and problem solving skills through carefully-designed instructional or enrichment programs. The Creative Learning Model has also been extended into a framework for program planning, called *Individualized Programming Planning Model* (*IPPM*). The IPPM approach provides a framework and resources for identification and program design, and has been implemented in several school districts (Treffinger, 1985).

Individualized Educational Programs (IEP) for the Gifted

Enrichment activities for gifted students in the regular classroom seemed not to produce measurable gains or advantages according to research cited earlier. However, new efforts to individualize and specify learning outcomes for the gifted show promise of overcoming the failures of general enrichment programs. Perhaps it is the required specificity of a learning contract as well as the learning objectives, both of which often characterize this approach, which may make the difference.

Feldhusen, Rand and Crowe (1975) described a system for individualizing instruction based on use of learning agreements and learning centers. The system individualizes instruction in several basic skills areas and classroom art activities. Children plan by the day or week according to activities which are listed on a chart as available. They can create their own order or sequence, proceed at their own rates, and emphasize certain areas over others. The system is uniquely successful with gifted children who have heightened capacity to read and learn independently. Gifted children can forge ahead in basic skills areas and in conceptual learning to higher levels appropriate to their abilities. The teacher watches each child's plan very carefully, urges modification to include more time on basic skills if necessary, and evaluates each child's progress. The teacher also meets with small groups for reading and project activities and with the whole class for some activities such as social studies, book reports and class discussions. Feldhusen (1981) has described the model in operational detail in a second grade heterogeneous classroom in which a cluster of gifted youth are given differentiated instructional activities. The students also receive a great deal of instruction and practice in self-guided, independent learning procedures.

Another individualized approach is Project UP (Unlimited Potential; Marion Community Schools, 1978). Students are identified by classroom teachers utilizing checklists for four areas: learning ability, motivation, leadership, and creativity. One resource teacher is needed at the elementary level and one at the secondary level to assist teachers in the identification process and in other activities to be described next. Project UP provides the checklist forms for identification.

Once the child has been identified as gifted a conference is arranged with the parents to explain the programs and to secure more information about the child. The child is also interviewed to assess his/her interests and to explain the program. Forms are provided for these interviews.

Each student then plans activities with assistance from the teacher and following lists of suggestions provided by Project UP. General suggestions are provided for activities, although they are sometimes quite vague. For example:

> Providing activities that cover a range of difficulty and the scope of complexity as they relate to a particular area or skill

> or

> Affording students with opportunities to avail themselves of expertise in the community

It is doubtful that such extremely vague statements would be of value to teachers; hopefully the resource teachers would have more concrete suggestions for activities.

Once an activity has been formulated a written statement is prepared and signed as a contract or agreement by the student, teacher, and parent. Once a project is completed, the teacher evaluates it and prepares a written report. The Project UP manual gives a list of reading and study resources and spells out the roles of the parents, teacher, and student quite precisely. This project offers one quite good framework for developing individual plans and activities for the gifted.

Treffinger (1979) offered specific recommendations for schools which are planning IEPs for gifted, creative and talented students.

1. Attention should be given to the unique talents and characteristics of each student using information from the cumulative folder and from the identification process.
2. The IEP should take into account the student's interests, motivation, and learning style.
3. The IEP goals should focus on basic skill learning, enrichment activities, acceleration when appropriate, fostering independence and self direction, experience in valuing, and personal development.
4. IEPs for the gifted should often explore the unknown and futuristic concerns.
5. There should be much experience in finding and solving problems, inquiry skills, and research methodology.
6. Gifted students should participate in the development of the IEP.
7. The IEP should provide for coordination of learning resources at school, at home, and in the community.
8. The IEP should serve to facilitate communication among the student, teacher, parents, and community resource persons regarding the student's program.
9. IEPs should be continuously monitored by the student, teacher, and parents and adapted as necessary.
10. There should be a good system of evaluation and record keeping with both students and teachers participating in the evaluation process.

These guidelines can provide excellent direction for schools which are developing individualized programs for the gifted. It is often the case that teachers may wish to use IEPs not only with gifted, creative, and talented students but also with the whole class. This may be potentially constructive, although caution must be exercised to minimize the possibility that the gifted, creative and talented will be "lost in the shuffle" and will engage in activities not really different from those pursued by less able peers. If the IEPs are to be used with the whole class we urge careful consideration of the model described by Feldhusen, Rand, and Crowe (1975). It affords a proven system for implementing all the guidelines offered by Treffinger (1979). If the IEPs are to be used only with the gifted, creative and talented, Project UP (Marion Public Schools, 1978) affords a practical model. However, the latter project offers little or no guidance concerning learning activities. For more specific direction to appropriate activities, the model described by Feldhusen and Kolloff 1978, 1979 and by OrRico and Feldhusen 1979 and Feldhusen, Hynes and Richardson (1977) offer concrete guidelines for the teacher. Guidance for effective planning of individualized instructional materials may be found in Treffinger, Hohn, and Feldhusen (1979). An additional model for developing IEPs for gifted and

NAME OF STUDENT _____

GRADE LEVEL _____ PERIOD COVERED _____

SPECIAL TALENTS, STRENGTHS

_____

_____

_____

WEAKNESSES, REMEDIAL NEEDS

_____

_____

_____

RECOMMENDED PROGRAM SERVICES OR OPTIONS

   SCHOOL RELATED _____

_____

_____

   EXTRA SCHOOL _____

_____

_____

SPECIFIC LEARNING OBJECTIVES

_____

_____

_____

RECOMMENDED EVALUATION CHECKPOINT

_____

_____

_____

Figure 2.5. Individualized Education Program

talented students is presented by Renzulli and Smith (1979; 1980). A model IEP for the gifted is presented in Figure 2.5.

Summary

This chapter focussed on methods and activities for teaching creative thinking and problem solving to gifted, creative and talented students. We have described several approaches, models, and systems which have been implemented with groups and individual gifted students. The authors have worked with many schools developing programs for the gifted. Programs can be developed to meet the individual needs of students by effectively using the resources of the teachers and the community.

Chapter 3

IMPLICATIONS OF MODELS FOR PLANNING AND INSTRUCTION FOR THE GIFTED AND TALENTED

In Chapter 2, we presented four models for developing enrichment and creative learning programs. Of course, these are not the *only* models for planning programs for gifted, talented, and creative students; Maker (1982) described ten general models that are widely used in program planning. The models we selected in Chapter 2 were those with which we have had the most experience and success in relation to the specific goals of enrichment and creativity. In this Chapter, we will consider the implications of those models for program planning and for instructional practice. We will begin with some general implications, which cut across subject areas and grade levels. Then we will describe some of the unique considerations at the elementary and secondary levels. In Chapter 4, we will describe specific ways to begin a program for enrichment and creative learning in your own classroom.

General Implications

There are many points on which there is considerable agreement among the models presented in Chapter 2, and which we consider important factors in planning or conducting effective programming at any grade level. These commonalities represent the most fundamental implications that should guide your decision-making from the very first steps in planning school programs.

1. "Giftedness" involves potential for creative productivity.

The importance of enrichment and creative learning in each of the models in Chapter 2 stems from the fact that creative abilities and skills are fundamental components of their view of "giftedness." In each model, giftedness includes the ability to learn and acquire information readily, but it also involves being able to generate ideas and to use information productively in complex thinking and problem solving tasks. In our view then, effective programs should specifically and deliberately incorporate strategies and activities that will foster the development of independent, creative learning among the students.

25

2. There should be flexibility in any identification process.

Each of these models acknowledges that independent, creative learning draws upon a variety of different strengths and characteristics of students. Many students exhibit potential for outstanding performance or accomplishment in one or more of a number of different fields or disciplines. In addition, strengths and talents previously unexpressed or undiscovered may emerge at different times or in response to encouragement, skillful instruction, and challenge. Finally, the number of students who can successfully and productively benefit from enrichment and creative learning cannot be arbitrarily set at any fixed percentage of a school population. These concerns lead us to the conclusion that considerable flexibility is essential in the identification process in any program for enrichment and creative learning. Identification should be *inclusive* (making efforts to recognize and respond to students' characteristics) rather than *exclusive* (deciding who can or should be excluded from a program).

3. Programming decisions should be drawn directly from identification data.

The most important function of data gathered during the identification process is *not* that they might be used to select a group of students, but that they might provide valuable information about the students' learning characteristics and hence offer insights into ways of improving instruction for them. By examining data about a student's achievement in a certain subject area, combined with data about the student's special interests, we can be more effective in developing appropriate activities. A student who has already mastered basic concepts of general science at a high level, for example, and who is interested in meteorology might be best served by activities that involve setting up and monitoring a weather station at home or at school, visiting or working with staff members from the local weather bureau or area radio or television weather forecasters, planning and conducting an original experiment, or taking advanced and specialized science courses, rather than being obliged to take a general science course that is prescribed for all students at a certain grade level. Effective programs for enrichment and creative learning should obtain and use information about students to assist teachers in recognizing students' strengths and thus improve our ability to provide effective, appropriate instruction.

4. Enrichment and creative learning involves instruction that builds upon students' strengths and interests.

When teachers become involved in programs for enrichment and creative learning, we believe they are making a commitment to build upon the most positive attributes and needs of their students. Instead of focussing primarily on students' deficiencies and weaknesses, trying to "fix up" the students, they will be challenging and encouraging students to capitalize and expand on their

26

strongest talents and interests and their preferred styles or ways of learning. This does not mean that *all* curriculum should be centered on student interests, nor that specific limitations of individual students should be ignored. Rather, we believe that these models challenge educators to create programs which will nurture strengths and stimulate growth—extending and expanding learning opportunities to build motivation, involvement, and success in all learning tasks.

5. Enrichment and creative learning begin with exploration and basic thinking skills and progress gradually towards involvement in real problems.

Each of these models emphasizes that instruction for enrichment and creativity should begin with learning the basic "tools" of divergent and convergent thinking and with opportunities to explore and pursue one's curiosity. Subsequently, more complex thinking and feeling processes can be addressed, and the student can practice applying the basic tools in realistic (if "contrived") situations. Such "practice problems" give the students opportunities to polish and improve their proficiency in using complex thinking skills and systems for problem solving. Eventually, the students will be prepared to apply those skills and systems in tackling real problems and challenges, and in working on projects on their own. Effective programs for enrichment and creative learning provide experiences and support that enable this gradual development of competence in independent creative learning to occur.

6. The role of the regular school program cannot and should not be overlooked or minimized.

In most public school settings, for the foreseeable future, efforts to develop programming for enrichment and creative learning will be undertaken as part of the students' total school experience. Much responsibility for daily instruction will continue to fall upon regular classroom teachers. Fortunately, many effective methods and activities for enrichment and creative learning can be conducted in the regular classroom. Strategies for critical and creative thinking, such as making inferences and deductions, thinking through analogies, brainstorming, and attribute listing can be linked to instruction in many basic content areas. Effective programs involve all classroom teachers in such efforts, and provide support, materials, and training for them.

7. The teacher's role in enrichment and creative learning should not be oversimplified as process facilitation "versus" content instruction.

It would be much too simple—and, we believe, quite incorrect—to suggest that in basic areas the teacher's role is one of presenting content or transmitting information, but that in enrichment and creative learning, the role changes to that of process guide or facilitator. To be sure, in working with students on independent projects and solving real problems, it is very impor-

27

tant for the teacher to be able to assume a facilitative role. But the important role of *instruction,* in content areas and in basic process "tools," should not be overlooked or underestimated. Effective programs recognize the need for a suitable balance between teaching and facilitation.

8. *Programming can be provided in a variety of ways and places, at different times, and by different human and material resources.*

There is not just one fixed way of providing enrichment and creative learning opportunities for all students. By virtue of the variety of talents and interests of students, teachers, and other resource people, effective programming should be open to serving the needs of different students in a variety of ways. In an effective school program, for example, the Future Problem Solving Program may be available to provide opportunities for some students to apply their creative thinking and problem solving abilities to dealing with future scenarios. Other students may be working together, with support and assistance from staff members, on "Odyssey of the Mind" problems, using their creativity and imagination in ways that involve inventing and constructing products to solve practical mechanical or design problems. Yet other students may be working on critical analysis of "Great Books," writing and producing an original play, creating a mural for the school, or creating and sharing new computer programs or software. All of these students, in the activities best suited to their strengths and talents, are involved in programming for enrichment and creative learning. Individual Educational Programs, as described in Chapter 2, can be a practical vehicle for integrating these experiences and for effective record-keeping for many students, and for organizing the cooperative planning efforts among classroom teachers and gifted education specialists.

9. *The regular curriculum can (and often does) serve as a springboard for enrichment and creative learning.*

We should not overlook ways in which topics within the regular curriculum can expose students to ideas, concepts, and experiences that are new and exciting to them. Good instruction in content areas challenges students to probe beyond the surface, to pose new questions, and to dig deeper or investigate new areas. Stimulating instructors are concerned with the trends and issues, the future and the "cutting edge," of their subjects, not merely with describing the present and past. Such challenges often provide effective beginnings for enrichment and creative learning. In addition, we must recognize the need for a broadening of our conception of "curriculum," in which the real problems in a field can be taken up by students through internships, practicum or field experiences, and mentor relationships. Appropriate acceleration, providing advanced content and topics, can stimulate students to consider new ideas and to deal with a richer, more complex "data base" from which they can draw in defining and investigating real problems.

28

10. Enrichment and creative learning are concerned with differentiation of students' responses, not merely with presentation of different curriculum materials.

Many creative thinking methods and activities can be used effectively by a wide variety of students, in different ways and towards different outcomes. As Gordon and Poze (1980) have documented effectively, creative learning methods such as Synectics can be used by some students to encourage or reinforce comprehension of basic concepts, and by other students as a starting point for enrichment, original expression, and extensive, independent investigation. The *technique* or material is not "differentiated;" the differentiation arises in the varying *responses* of the students. Much writing about "qualitative differentiation" for gifted students seems to be concerned only with looking for (or writing) different materials. In fact, we believe, it is much more important and powerful to consider the responses of the students, or the kinds and levels of thinking we are challenging them to do with any of the material we use. Teachers should not settle for too little from students; the high degree of challenge and stimulation involved in enrichment and creative learning is not attained simply by selecting different materials to present to the students. Effective programs for enrichment and creative learning should be alert to *student responses* that are unique, unusual, more complex or abstract, more fluent, or elaborative, or that contain the "seeds" for more extensive research

Elementary Programs

Many opportunities exist for programs that provide for enrichment and creative learning at the elementary school level. Among these, several can involve the regular classroom program (Treffinger, 1982a). Exploratory activities, such as field trips, guest speakers, media presentations, and interest development centers, are examples of activities that can be conducted in the regular school program. In addition, all teachers can incorporate opportunities for creative and critical thinking and other "higher level" thinking skills (such as the upper levels of Bloom's Taxonomy) into their instruction on a day-to-day basis. Differences among students in learning styles, preferences, and interests can be assessed or observed and used as a foundation for individualized planning and differentiated activities or assignments. At the elementary level, where the teacher is likely to be working with a class of twenty to thirty children throughout the school day, many of these activities can be readily implemented through the use of learning centers, learning stations, and contracts or learning agreements (e.g., Blackburn & Powell, 1976; Dunn & Dunn, 1972, 1975, 1978). Classroom space and materials can be used in a flexible way to provide for a variety of activities, and displays or bulletin boards can easily be incorporated into planning a varied and stimulating learning environment.

It is widely recognized, however, that students with academic or creative ability or other specific strengths and talents often place demands on the classroom teacher that seem to be very difficult for one person to meet, especially with limited resources and large, heterogeneous groups. It would be unrealistic to expect a single teacher to provide everything that might be needed to offer every student the best possible program each day, tailored exactly to his or her unique needs.

Many elementary schools have therefore developed special programs to supplement or augment the efforts of the regular program. In theory, at least, these programs should expand or extend the services that can be provided by the classroom teacher, rather than duplicating them. In practice, however, it has often been the case that such programs (for a variety of reasons) offer students opportunities to learn and practice critical and creative thinking skills, exploratory activities, and projects based on students' interests. We hope that, in the near future, efforts will increase to assist regular classroom teachers and special program teachers or coordinators to plan and carry out their work in an integrated, mutually supportive way. The IEP approach described in Chapter 2 may be a very important component of such efforts, since an individual plan for a student requires input and discussion among all those who will be working with the student. The IEP can serve as the vehicle through which communication is initiated, as well as a convenient method of summarizing and monitoring the decisions that are made.

Special programs to supplement or extend the regular program at the elementary level most commonly include cluster grouping, itinerant or consulting teacher services, and resource or "pull out" programs. The cluster approach brings together a number of students with similar strengths and talents into a single classroom. This "cluster" of students may be as small as three or four pupils in a particular classroom. The presence of such a cluster in the class presumably enables the teacher to plan specific activities and experiences for those students more effectively than might be possible if there were only one or two such students in each of several different classrooms. In addition, the presence of several students in the classroom who may share similar interests and needs should create more opportunities for students to interact with each other at a high level, thus motivating and challenging each other more than might be possible if they were alone in a heterogeneous class. It is not entirely clear that, when clusters are formed on the basis of global indicators (such as IQ scores), as commonly occurs, such an exchange of ideas and interests will actually be found, but in practice, it does seem that some teachers *feel* more comfortable or confident in working with enrichment and creative learning when such a cluster is present. In this approach, it may also be possible to address teachers' training needs more efficiently, since there will be a smaller number of "cluster" teachers with whom to work, rather than to try to help *every* teacher learn how to deal with the unique needs and characteristics of gifted, talented, and creative students. Finally, when financial limitations restrict opportunities to purchase supplementary or enrichment materials, cluster groups may offer a cost-efficient approach to resource acquisition and distribution.

Itinerant or consulting teacher models can involve a variety of different degrees and kinds of services. In some settings, for example, one itinerant teacher may be expected to serve a large number of different buildings on some kind of "rotating" schedule. This might involve meeting with students in any particular building for special activities and experiences only on a very infrequent basis. Some programs may involve as little as one half-day once or twice a month, for example. In such a situation, it is extremely difficult for the itinerant teacher to develop and carry out activities with substance and continuity, and it may be virtually impossible for the itinerant teacher to coordinate or communicate at all with the classroom teachers in any building. Consequently, the "program" is often a series of isolated, brief exercises or activities which the teacher hopes will provide extra challenge or thinking skills that might transfer to other school learning activities. In other settings, the itinerant teacher may spend as much as one half-day each week with various groups of students. This may allow for the development of more complex activities and projects during the course of a school year, but opportunities for coordination with classroom teachers may still be very limited or even nonexistent. In a few situations, the teacher may serve a smaller number of buildings and may also be provided with time and opportunities to meet with classroom teachers for cooperative planning and sharing of resources. If this model is employed, such provisions are highly desirable.

In some programs, particularly those following the IPPM (Individualized Program Planning Model) approach (Treffinger, 1981, 1985a) or aspects of Renzulli, Reis & Smith's (1981) "Revolving Door" model, a gifted education specialist may work with a smaller number of buildings, or even within a single building, and be expected not only to work directly with students but also to serve as a resource or "consultant" for other teachers on a regular basis.

The resource room or "pull out" program is by far the most common method of providing special programs at the elementary level (Gallagher, Weiss, Oglesby, and Thomas, 1983). Again this approach may be implemented in a number of different ways. The most common way is for a group of students to be identified as gifted, talented, or creative and to provide special activities or experiences for them away from the regular classroom, usually in a separate room in the building (a "resource room") at a designated time each week. This approach is similar to special resource room programs in remedial subject areas or for handicapped students. Although the "pull out" approach is familiar in the school, and can often be implemented with efficiency in cost and time, it also has a number of significant potential liabilities. Learning experiences for students in the pull out program may be fragmented or isolated from the content and curriculum of the regular program. This may also lead to teacher nonsupport or even hostility towards the separate pro-

31

gram, and to competition for the student's interest and attention between the regular and pull out programs. There may also be a danger of labelling and creating certain affective difficulties and expectations within the students themselves, their peers, their families, or their teachers. The pull out program model may also contribute to the notion that there is one, single identifiable group of gifted students, and that their needs can be met by a single program; these are assumptions that are strongly questioned by the models of enrichment and creative learning presented in Chapter Two, and in other sources such as a special issue of the *Gifted Child Quarterly* (Fall 1982; volume 26, Number 1) on "demythologizing" gifted education. Even excellent, stimulating pull out programs may risk heightening the contrast with the regular program and increasing frustration or boredom for students. The time given to pull out programs is typically so small, often only two or three hours a week, that it can become only a "patch on" time for entertainment, puzzles, games, or isolated activities (Treffinger, 1982b). A stimulating discussion of some of the strengths and weaknesses of pull out programs has been provided by Cox and Daniel (1984).

Some resource programs use a special "center" approach in which students from several buildings may be transported regularly to a special program which meets in a central location, for time periods typically ranging from a half-day to one full day per week. It is common, for example, for students at specific grade levels from the "feeder" schools to go to the center at a particular time each week. These programs may offer some efficiency in relation to staffing and centralization of resources and materials. But they increase the isolation of the gifted program effort from other aspects of the student's total educational program, highlight the departure of a certain group of students from the building each week, and involve considerable need for complex planning and budgeting for transportation.

In the "Revolving Door" apprach (Renzulli et al., 1981) the resource room is a central component of the program, but it functions differently than in other pull out models. Rather than selecting a single, fixed group of students who will participate in resource room activities throughout the school year, the gifted education teacher draws students to a resource room for specific purposes and variable time periods. Students participate in resource room activities to obtain assistance in planning, conducting, evaluating, and sharing specific investigations of real problems (Type III projects, in the language of Renzulli's Enrichment Triad model, described in Chapter 2). Students may be referred to the resource room for assistance and support in such activities as learning advanced research or methodological skills, locating and using appropriate resource materials and people, carrying out independent investigative activities, developing products, and locating appropriate audiences or outlets for their work. For some students and projects, this may require only a few days, but for others it may involve extensive time and effort over several weeks or months. This approach avoids some of the common problems associated with pull out models, but must still deal with complex issues relating to scheduling, communication among staff members, and coordinating activities to insure continuity and challenge in the student's entire school program.

In considering the resource room approach, it may be important for us to begin to distinguish between "pull out" and "pull in" concepts. Rather than designating a single group of students for a single, fixed program, emphasizing pulling them *out* of their regular program, it may be much more desirable to think about recognizing the need to pull some students *in* (i.e., draw them together) on the basis of their common needs and interests. Gifted education specialists and classroom teachers may be able to work together much more effectively by making deliberate efforts to focus on the specific needs of the students and asking, "In what ways might we provide appropriate activities and services to meet the student's needs?"

Special, Full-Time Classes for Gifted Students

There is growing interest among schools throughout the United States in organizing special, full-time, self-contained classes for gifted youngsters. There are at least three reasons for this. First, the needs of many of these gifted youngsters are not being met in regular classrooms; second, pullout programs often fail to provide for the academic needs of these youngsters; and third, the special full-time, self-contained classes offer a more cost effective approach than pullout classes.

Gallagher et. al. did a survey (1983) of gifted programs in the United States and got 1200 responses to a questionnaire which asked about preferred program models. The most popular model was the resource-room/pullout-program model (41%), but special classes were second most preferred (23%). Enrichment in the regular classroom was selected by 10% of respondents. Gallagher also found that special classes cost somewhat less than resource-room/pullout-program classes. Gallagher noted that special classes are most popular in grades 3–6. Very few are offered at the primary level. At the junior high or middle school level and at the high school level advanced or honors classes are the most popular mode of instruction for highly able students.

Children in these classes are often mainstreamed for art, music, physical education and/or social studies to promote their social interaction with average and less able children. There is no evidence of deficient social learning among children in special classes, but the mainstreaming movement in special education has served to create an equal concern for highly able children in special classes.

There is not much research on the effect of special classes for the gifted, but a few excellent studies have been done. Martinson's study (1961) was probably one of the largest ever done to assess the effects of different modes of providing for the gifted; 17 program models were evaluated. For each model an experimental and a control group was organized. She found that special classes produced superior achievement gains for these youngsters and no negative effects on social relationships. Observations indicated that the special teachers did an excellent job of teaching these youngsters in special classes, and the teachers reported a very high degree of satisfaction in teaching gifted classes.

In 1969 Bent et al. reported on an excellent and well designed study in which 366 gifted children were grouped in special classes beginning at grade three. They stayed in such classes to grade eight. Each child was matched with a control group partner on the basis of ability and socioeconomic status. They found that children in special classes were superior to controls in academic achievement, knowledge of a foreign language, research skills, thinking skills, writing ability, social awareness, breadth of interests, and self reliance. Teachers and parents were very favorable in their evaluation of these special classes.

Schreffler also reported research (1969) on special classes for the gifted. A special class was organized at the 6th grade level and compared with two control groups of gifted youngsters who were not in special classes. Children in special classes scored higher on school grades, participation in extracurricular activities and leadership. However, the higher academic achievement tended to decrease by grade 12 because many of the children were not able to continue in special classes after grade six. Renzulli did a study (1972) of three programs for the gifted in the area of Providence, Rhode Island. One program involved special classes in grades 4–6 while the other two programs were pullout models. The results showed that all three models were highly successful and produced higher academic achievement. Evans reported (1978) on a new program for highly gifted children enrolled in a magnet school. Three groups were used: (1) children bussed to a magnet school, (2) children organized in special classes in their regular school, and (3) a control group who were not in any special classes. He found that minority students improved their academic performance when they were enrolled in the magnet school, but the other children in special classes simply stayed at the same level of academic performance. However, this finding that children maintained their academic performance (without declining as they advanced in grade) did constitute a program advantage.

Kulik and Kulik recently reviewed (1982) 52 studies on ability grouping at the secondary level. They found that special classes generally had beneficial effects on the academic achievement of gifted and talented students, that there were no negative effects on the achievement of children in average and low ability classes, and that students attitudes toward school and self concept were more favorable in grouped classes.

Barbe (1957) carried out a long range (15 years) followup of 456 students who had been in special classes in the Cleveland Major Work Program. He found that the performance and achievements of these people in adulthood were decidedly superior to the general population. Their interests were broad, they were socially well adjusted, and they were very active in community and school affairs.

We conclude from this review that the needs of highly able children are not fully satisfied in regular classrooms, that special classes with well trained teachers can produce superior achievement, that gifted and talented children will develop superior thinking skills and broader interests in special classes, and that social adjustment and learning will not be impaired for any children when special classes are organized. However, it seems clear that these teachers of special classes need special training in how to teach higher level thinking skills such as creative thinking, problem solving, analysis, synthesis, evaluation, logic, and critical thinking and that they need to know how to use instructional materials which are especially designed to facilitate teaching of thinking skills.

In a special class for the gifted there should be ample time to focus on the teaching of thinking skills and often to be able to embed the teaching of those skills in the teaching of mathematics, science, social studies and English. There is a frequent complaint that creativity and other thinking skills are often taught in isolation in pullout/resource room programs and that children will not learn how to transfer or use the skills in the basic disciplines and in realistic learning situations. The teacher of a special class must deal with instruction in English or language arts, reading, science, social studies and mathematics. Active, interactive or generative learning in these areas calls for inquiry, experimentation, discovery, investigation, hypothesizing, creating and evaluating. Thus, the teacher of special classes for the gifted should be able to foster a dynamic growth in thinking skill in gifted youth.

Special Concerns in the Primary Grades

Programs for enrichment and creative learning for students in the primary grades present a number of special concerns. Young children, especially those entering Kindergarten, are new at being away from home, and time will be required for them to feel comfortable in the new environment presented by the school. Similarly, time will be required for teachers to observe the students in a number of different situations and to become aware of their unique characteristics, strengths, and talents. Parent information and input can provide very useful data (if it addresses the specific behavior and accomplishments of the child, rather than merely global categorizing of the student as "gifted"). Much early assessment must be individual and often informal or anecdotal. Younger students also need a rich, stimulating environment with many opportunities for exploration and discovery, opportunities to express themselves in many ways, and challenges that provide a foundation for effective thinking and study skills in later years. Hazel Feldhusen (1981) described an approach to classroom organization and instructional management in the regular classroom in which there is considerable challenge and stimulation for gifted, talented, and creative young students.

Secondary Programs

Some aspects of secondary education lend themselves very naturally and easily to programming for enrichment and creative learning. In many secondary schools, for example, a number of programming options are already available for students, both within the curriculum and through a wide range of clubs, activities, and extracurricular programs. Faculty members are specialists in their own content areas, and most departments include some very talented individuals who are actively involved in current developments in their disciplines. Many content-related instructional options (advanced courses, honors programs, Advanced Placement, etc.) may already be offered or are readily available through nationally-known programs, and there are often opportunities for students to co-enroll in courses at area community colleges or universities. Students' talents may be expressed in more specific or differentiated ways, which can offer the potential for more appropriate and effective identification procedures for programming involving many options.

At the same time, however, there are many factors that can inhibit the development and implementation of programming for enrichment and creative learning at the secondary level. Both teachers and students may be spread very thin: teachers with many preparations, serving 125–150 students each day; students with increasing pressures and requirements for daily assignments and graduation, and with commitments to many outside activities. Scheduling problems can be very complex, since each student's daily program brings him or her into contact with a number of different people and places. Graduation and credit requirements may mandate so many hours of instruction in basic areas that even the most highly talented and motivated students are forced to weigh what they *want* to do against what they are *required* to do. Finally, some teachers may view themselves as presenters of a fixed set of information and ideas in a single content area, and may risk losing sight of the individual strengths, characteristics, needs or interests of students. Thus, secondary education is an area of both "plenty" and "poverty" in programming for gifted, talented, and creative students.

Secondary programs for enrichment and creative learning are usually quite different from elementary programs. The ubiquitous pull out or resource room model of the elementary level will seldom be found at the secondary level. In accord with the increasing specialization of students' areas of talent and interests, secondary programs are more likely to be differentiated by specific content areas (mathematics, science, social studies, etc.). Within subject areas, there is usually a strong emphasis on the importance of *content* instruction, and provisions for enrichment and creative learning must develop within this context, rather than with the specific "process orientation" that is commonly found at the elementary level.

Keating (1979) discussed approaches to secondary programming, and urged strongly that identification and programming should be related to students' specific aptitudes and talents. Special classes, which might provide opportunities for both acceleration and enrichment, were recommended as a major approach at the secondary level. This suggestion was echoed by the findings of Gallagher et al. (1983), whose survey found that special, advanced classes in subject matter areas were the preferred and most common programming mode at this level. Milne (1982) described the role of vocational education in the lives of gifted and talented students and the needs of students with special talents and interests in vocational areas. He reported (from a conference of 300 vocational educators) that youth whose talents and creativity are expressed in these areas are seldom identified, and that, despite the availability of many excellent programs in these areas, such students frequently are not adequately served by counseling or by programs.

An essential component of any effective secondary enrichment or creative learning effort should be special career education services. Getzels and Jackson (1962) reported that highly creative students were often uninterested in traditional career opportunities, preferring instead to explore or even to create unique and unusual career possibilities for themselves. The rapid pace of change in our world, and the major transitions such as those described by Naisbitt (1982), also suggest that gifted, talented, and creative students will need flexible guidance and support in analyzing their needs, interests, and possible career directions. Kerr (1981) suggested that gifted and talented youth experience three major problems in career decision-making: (1) how to decide on a career direction when one's talents are multiple and varied; (2) attaining emotional maturity to match their intellectual or artistic precocity; and (3) coping with societal demands and expectations of the gifted person. She described a number of program models to consider, involving mentoring, special career education classes, counseling, and summer career exploration programs. Skills in critical thinking, creative thinking, and problem solving may be especially important to adolescents in dealing effectively with these challenges. Moore, Feldhusen, and Owings (1978) reported results of a career exploration-education program which offered gifted, talented, and creative youth experiences in a mentor program and career education seminar. They found the experiences very valuable in helping youth to clarify their career goals and plans and to stimulate their interest and increase their aspirations in career planning. Torrance (1984) also described many of the benefits of mentor relationships for gifted and creative individuals, and outlined several ways in which the *absence* of a mentor relationship might serve to impair or inhibit creative, productive development and expression. Juntune (1981) described 69 junior high school and 40 high school programs for gifted, talented, and creative youth, many of which involved mentoring, special classes, future studies, leadership development, IEPs and independent study options.

Feldhusen and Reilly (1983) described a model for secondary programs in which provisions are made for many options and services to promote content mastery and advanced learning as well as enrichment and creative learning. They began by suggesting that secondary programs should provide a number

Elementary Services	Junior High or Middle School Services	High School Services
1. Full-Time Classes	1. Counselling	1. Counselling
2. Pullout Classes	2. Accelerated Classes	2. Advance Placement Courses
3. Junior Great Books	3. Future Problem Solving	3. Accelerated Classes
4. Future Problem Solving	4. Junior Great Books	4. Foreign Language
5. Olympics of the Mind	5. Olympics of the Mind	5. Seminar
6. Careers Exploration	6. Career Education	6. Independent Study
7. Mentors	7. Seminar	7. Mentors
8. Saturday Classes	8. Individual Tutors or Mentors	8. College Courses
9. Summer Opportunities	9. AP or College Classes Open to Some	9. Career Education
10. Foreign Language— Exploratory Study	10. Higher Math Classes Open	10. Correspondence Study
11. Grade Advancement	11. Foreign Language	11. Opportunities in Arts and Humanities
	12. Opportunities in Art, Music, Drama and Dance	

Figure 3.1. Serious programs for the gifted

of services which are articulated with and planned continuations of elementary programs. Figure 3.1 shows an illustrative set of services which might be offered at each level (elementary, junior high school, high school). Identification processes should stress recognition of particular areas of talent, not just global indicators of ability. Students may vary widely in their abilities in different content areas, and should not be expected to demonstrate exceptional performance in *every* area!

Appropriate services should be planned for each student, using a planning guide such as the one illustrated in Figure 3.2, called a "Growth Plan." The plan may be developed cooperatively by teacher(s), the counselor, and/or the gifted program director, and reviewed with the student and his or her family. The Growth Plan may include both in-school and extra-school experiences.

Figure 3.3 presents a more comprehensive secondary model. This is an attempt to specify all of the areas in which a program should provide services. Counselors should be involved in the identification process and in the devel-

Name _____ Phone __(   )_____

Grade Level _____

Current Courses _____

Athletics _____

Clubs, Organizations _____

Awards, Honors _____

Test Scores _____

Prior Experience in Gifted Program _____

Prior Research Experiences _____

Interest Analysis _____

Learning Styles _____

Students Own Goals	Recommended Classes for Next Year
Recommended Activities in School	Recommended Extra School Activities

Final Plan _____

_____

_____

_____

_____

Figure 3.2. Growth plan

opment of growth plans for each gifted student. Some gifted youth have personal problems which call for personal counselling, but a large part of the counselling service should be delivered to small groups of gifted youth in small group counselling sessions with 12–16 students. These sessions can focus on career opportunities, educational routes to those opportunities, methods of career decision making, understanding self and one's own talents and abilities, and adjusting to other people (gifted and non-gifted). Such small group counselling sessions for gifted and talented youth are conducted once a week by counsellors at Fulton Junior High School in Indianapolis, Indiana. The pro-

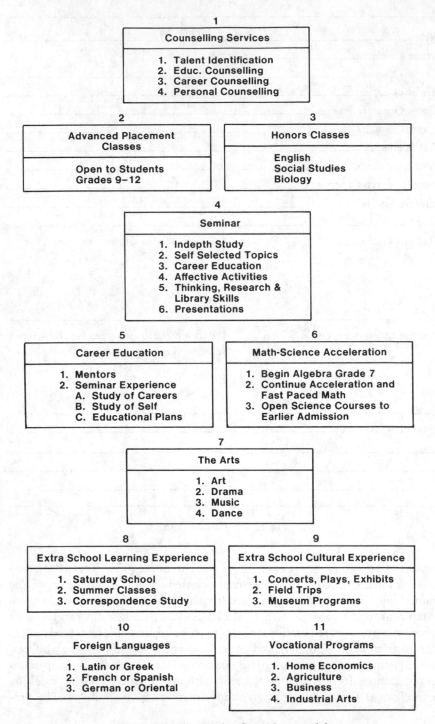

1

Counselling Services

1. Talent Identification
2. Educ. Counselling
3. Career Counselling
4. Personal Counselling

2

Advanced Placement Classes

Open to Students
Grades 9–12

3

Honors Classes

English
Social Studies
Biology

4

Seminar

1. Indepth Study
2. Self Selected Topics
3. Career Education
4. Affective Activities
5. Thinking, Research & Library Skills
6. Presentations

5

Career Education

1. Mentors
2. Seminar Experience
   A. Study of Careers
   B. Study of Self
   C. Educational Plans

6

Math-Science Acceleration

1. Begin Algebra Grade 7
2. Continue Acceleration and Fast Paced Math
3. Open Science Courses to Earlier Admission

7

The Arts

1. Art
2. Drama
3. Music
4. Dance

8

Extra School Learning Experience

1. Saturday School
2. Summer Classes
3. Correspondence Study

9

Extra School Cultural Experience

1. Concerts, Plays, Exhibits
2. Field Trips
3. Museum Programs

10

Foreign Languages

1. Latin or Greek
2. French or Spanish
3. German or Oriental

11

Vocational Programs

1. Home Economics
2. Agriculture
3. Business
4. Industrial Arts

Figure 3.3. The Purdue Secondary model

gram evaluations show it to be highly successful in meeting affective, social and career education needs of gifted and talented youth.

A second area of program services appears in blocks two, three, and six of Figure 3.3, namely special classes which may afford enriched and accelerated learning experiences as well as the opportunity to be challenged and to develop high level thinking and research skills. Honors classes in basic subject matters, College Board Advanced Placement courses for college credit, and acceleration which permits gifted youth to take courses in mathematics, science, foreign language, English or social studies ahead of schedule can afford all these special benefits. They help gifted youth avoid the inevitable boredom which otherwise besets them, sustain interest and motivation to learn, and foster valuable study methods and attitudes. Teachers of such courses must know how to use inquiry and problem-solving methods, and be adept at integrating instruction in thinking skills into their teaching. Research reviewed recently by Kulik and Kulik (1982) shows clearly that grouping bright students for special accelerated instruction with emphasis on higher level thinking skills leads to increased achievement and better attitudes-motivation toward school.

A third area of program service may be developed through a combination of concepts in boxes 4, 5 and 9, namely a seminar for the gifted which incorporates opportunities for a small group of gifted youth, working with a teacher, to engage in indepth study, have opportunities to share their research through presentations, develop higher level thinking skills, pursue career education goals, and engage in cultural learning experiences. The seminar usually consists of 12–16 gifted youth who meet during a scheduled period, carry on their research outside of class, and meet to present and discuss their research. The career education aspect may involve scheduled speakers, study of higher level occupations, and educational planning. The world of art and culture involved a realm of aesthetic experience and ideas which is unique and should be available to all gifted youth. Field trips to plays, concerts and art exhibits should be followed with discussion in seminar of the experience. The seminar can be the major opportunity for gifted youth to experience the joy of interaction with other gifted youth.

Good secondary programs identify youth who are talented in art, music, drama and dance (Box 7) and seek to provide opportunities for them in school or in the community. A number of cities have developed centers in the secondary program for the arts. New Orleans Center for the Creative Arts is such an example. Youngsters who are talented in the arts may not be discovered if there is no formal identification process in school. Identification in the arts is no more complicated nor less reliable than identification in the academic areas, but it does often involve product evaluation or audition. Some schools argue that the regular art, drama and music programs will identify and provide for these students. To some extent that may be true, but militating against that assertion is the lack of systematic identification and the preoccupation with providing opportunities for all youth, not just the talented. A separate effort is needed for the highly talented in art.

The area of foreign language study (Box 10) is especially critical for gifted youth as has been well recognized in the International Baccalaureate program (Phillips, 1982). Some exploratory study of foreign language(s) should begin for gifted youth in the elementary school. Serious, formal study should begin no later than the seventh grade. Gifted youth need foreign language study to enlarge their world views, to develop their growth of language structures, and to develop study skills and discipline. Learning a foreign language is an enriching experience also because the student learns a great deal about another culture. Thus, it seems to be imperative that all secondary gifted programs plan for the systematic study of foreign languages.

Many youth develop and exhibit their talent in the areas represented by vocational subjects—eg business, industrial arts, home economics, agriculture (Box 11). The criticism that gifted programs are elitist is probably exacerbated by our failure to recognize talent in the vocational areas. Vocational teachers are already well tuned to detecting-identifying youth who have special talent in their areas, and they have skill in devising individualized projects for those students. Milne (1982) provides further guidelines for the development of programs in this area. There may be little need for special seminars or pullout programs for the talented in the vocational areas. Excellent resources and activities may already exist. The important issue may be that of recognizing talent in this area as a part of the gifted program in a school.

Finally the education of secondary gifted and talented youth calls for a variety of experiences beyond school, notably in special Saturday and summer programs (Box 8). These programs, often based at colleges and universities, but also found in schools or operated by parent associations, offer gifted and talented youth an opportunity to study specialized topics, not commonly offered in school, with expert teachers-mentors and another opportunity for gifted youth to interact with other gifted youth. Feldhusen and Sokol (1982) described the Purdue Super Saturday program for gifted youth and Feldhusen and Clinkenbeard (1982) reviewed summer type programs for these students. There is some evaluation research which indicates that such programs are effective in helping meet the needs of gifted and talented youth.

Many of these options provide for learning that is not accelerative in relation to content, but also valuable as a basis for enrichment and creativity. Effective secondary programming should help students to refine and improve creative and critical thinking abilities, and to learn to apply problem solving methods and systems in dealing with a variety of complex issues and topics. Applications of those problem solving methods to real problems and challenges, by individuals or groups, can also be an important component, which can often be provided through special seminars or independent study.

Renzulli et al. (1981) have also proposed a secondary adaptation of their Revolving Door approach, in which special sections of core courses (basic academic subject areas) are provided for students who are part of a "talent pool." The talent pool students may enroll in one or more of these classes, depending on their interests and abilities. It is *not* expected that students will enroll in these special sections in *all* core subject areas. These courses may provide basic instruction at a faster rate or pace than regular classes, by virtue of the students' abilities and interests, but Renzulli et al. stress that they must also do more than "covering more content, faster." These courses should also provide (using the language of Renzulli's Enrichment Triad Model, described in Chapter 2) opportunities for Type I and Type II Enrichment (exploratory activities and training in methodological skills and techniques). The faster pace of the courses also provides opportunities to "buy time" for students to begin work on Type III Enrichment (individual or small group investigations of real problems). Renzulli et al. also recommend that, at the secondary level, there should be a multi-disciplinary planning committee, whose responsibilities include creating and offering many Type I activities and assisting students in Type III investigations.

An individualized approach proposed by Treffinger (1985b) also emphasizes the need for secondary programs to offer many different options for students and to insure that the students are effectively "linked" to the most appropriate alternatives for their needs. This model emphasizes opportunities that can be created in six important aspects of the school program: individualizing basic skills, effective acceleration, appropriate enrichment, independence and self direction, personal growth and social development, and career orientation with a futuristic perspective. Illustrations of representative options at the secondary level for each of these six areas are given in Figure 3.4.

Summary

In this chapter, we have attempted to describe the most important implications of the models described in Chapter 2 for identification and programming for enrichment and creative learning. We have also attempted to describe some specific concerns of particular importance for elementary and secondary education. It is essential, we believe, that effective programming for enrichment and creative learning for gifted, talented, and creative students be *flexible* and *diverse* in recognizing and responding to students' unique strengths and talents.

Individualized Basics	Learning Styles
	Individualized Unit Planning
	Test Out/Credit By Examination
	Mini-Courses
	Multidisciplinary Studies
	Academic Competitions
	Thinking Skills Instruction
	Courses, Seminars, Workshops
Effective Acceleration	Off-level Testing, Talent Search
	Advanced Placement, I-B Program
	Test Out/Credit By Examination
	College Courses—dual enrollment
	Early College Admission
	MENSA—Other Personal Support Groups
	Scheduling Assistance ("Ombudsman")
Appropriate Enrichment	Type I—Speakers, Trips, Colloquia
	Type II—Thinking Skills, CPS
	Seminars, Electives, Mini-Courses
	Mentorships, Internships
	Research Investigations/Indepen. Study
	Extra or Co-Curricular, Clubs
	Summer, Evening, Saturday Classes
	Community Resource or Service Programs
	Governor's School, Special-Residential
	Competitions and Bowls

Figure 3.4. Illustrative programming methods and resources at the secondary level

Independence and Self-Direction	Research Seminar/Study Skills Contracts/Independent Study Locating & Using Resources Internships and Mentorship Teaching in program for adults or for younger students Get involved in outside research projects Community group participation Enter Competition for Talent/ Achievements Junior Achievement Programs/FFA, etc. Become an expert on some topic!
Personal Growth and Social Development	Leadership Experiences Group dynamics exercises Individual and Group Counseling Valuing—dealing with talents and respecting differences Understanding Learning Styles Competence in social settings—finding "true peers."
Career Perspectives and a Futuristic Orientation	Bibliotherapy—Reading about Models Shadowing experiences Future Problem Solving Courses, Seminars, and Units on Changes, futures Individual Planning and Goal-setting Experiences and Skills Designing a career

Source: Treffinger (1985b)

Figure 3.4—*Continued*

Chapter 4

METHODS OF TEACHING CREATIVITY AND PROBLEM SOLVING

You should not be content to wait for creativity and problem solving to occur "spontaneously" in teaching the gifted. If you really want to emphasize goals that involve fostering these thinking processes, it will be necessary for you to take some very direct, deliberate action to see that it happens!

In this chapter, we shall review some of the methods and techniques that you can use in your classroom to stimulate creative thinking and problem solving. They are not "tricks" or "games" that are ends in themselves, of course, and they can be utilized as you are carrying out your regular, day-to-day instruction in language arts, social studies, or almost any other subject area. In fact, creativity is probably taught most effectively in the context of a discipline or subject matter.

Each of the sections of this chapter will deal with an aspect of the problem that has been widely-studied and written about. Our purpose is not to provide a detailed explanation and scholarly criticism of the method, but merely to provide you with an introduction to illustrate some useful techniques that can be applied by any teacher working with gifted students.

Fostering a Creative Classroom Climate

Creativity can be viewed as a process of change in thinking and action. The combination of ideas, previously unconnected, into a novel idea or concept requires change. In order to foster creativity in your classroom, it is necessary to create an atmosphere that is receptive to new ideas. A positive, reinforcing, accepting climate is the basic ingredient necessary for the nurturance of creative behavior. Many obstacles to creative thinking are emotional reactions to insecure feelings which are caused by fear of new or different ideas. By suggesting novel ideas people open themselves to criticism. It is often easier to conform to the norm than taking the risk of expressing a novel idea or thought. New or different ideas can flourish in an open system, one that is flexible and oriented towards the individual student. In such an atmosphere, the emphasis rests on the student's interests and ideas. This can be accomplished by creating a climate of mutual respect and acceptance between students and teacher.

It is sometimes difficult to be creative because of learned attitudes. These atttitudes are often expressed by statements such as "I have a mental block against math" or "I'm not very good at solving puzzles." Blocks in thought patterns which inhibit creative thinking may be caused by perception or emotion.

By encouraging and reinforcing unusual ideas, students' attitudes can be positively directed towards a willingness to think and experiment with new ideas. Continued support and positive attitudes from the teacher are the fuel necessary to power the positive motivational climate that will set the stage for a creative atmosphere. An environment of adaptation to individual pupil's needs and interests, willingness to modify and vary planned activities in the interest and support of the students, and emphasis on divergent thinking skills will result in a warm and spontaneous climate which will spawn creativity.

Here are some general suggestions for creating an atmosphere conducive to creative thinking:

1. Support and reinforce unusual ideas and responses of students.
2. Use failure as a positive opportunity to help students realize errors and meet acceptable standards in a supportive atmosphere.
3. Adapt classroom procedures to student interests and ideas whenever possible.
4. Allow time for students to think about and develop their creative ideas. Not all creativity occurs immediately and spontaneously.
5. Create a climate of mutual respect and acceptance between students and between students and teachers, so that students can share, develop, and learn together and from one another as well as independently.
6. Be aware of the many facets of creativity besides arts and crafts: verbal responses, written responses both in prose and poetic style, fiction and nonfiction form. Creativity can be expressed in all curricular areas and disciplines.
7. Encourage divergent learning activities. Be a resource provider and director. Encourage students to explore alternatives.
8. Listen and laugh with students. A warm supportive atmosphere provides freedom and security in exploratory thinking.
9. Allow students to make choices and be a part of the decision-making process. Let them have a part in the control of their education and learning experiences.
10. Let everyone get involved, and demonstrate the value of involvement by supporting student ideas and solutions to problems and projects.

Inquiry, Discovery, Problem Solving and Creativity

Problem solving is the process of recognizing an obstacle, difficulty, or inability to act; thinking of possible solutions; and testing or evaluating the solutions. The inquiry, or discovery, approach to learning has been labeled the complete problem-solving process. This approach has the unique advantage of making a learning experience meaningful to the individual learner.

The process of inquiry begins when individuals question something in their experience. The teacher can structure students' learning experiences in such a way that they will question. Once they begin to inquire, intrinsic interest is stimulated and a learning by discovery process takes place.

There are three phases involved in the inquiry problem-solving process. The first is awareness, sensing that a problem exists. This is the motivating factor which arouses the student to go further in defining and resolving a problem. Once the problem is brought into awareness, the problem formulating stage begins. During this phase the problem is defined and ideas arise for plausible solution strategies. It is during this phase that information about the problem is gathered, usually through inquiry behavior such as reading, questioning, and trial-and-error behavior. The next stage is searching. During this period questioning and information gathering begin to be associated with the formulation of viable hypotheses. Backtracking to reconsider and recapitulation may occur in this phase.

When all necessary information has been gathered and a plausible hypothesis has been formulated and tested, the problem solvers may feel the problem has been resolved. The answers to inquiry procedures may not always be a product of the same inferences and generalizations, even within the same manipulative situation, for the inquiry process is unique to each student's questioning pursuits and interests. The inquiry approach is necessarily a divergent thinking technique. Each student will approach the problem with a unique background of experience and focus and direct activities towards goals that are individually real and meaningful.

Inquiry techniques work well in the classroom in which a warm, open classroom atmosphere prevails. Conditions that foster creativity will also promote inquiry, for students involved in a discovery process must feel free to combine new ideas, ask questions, share their thoughts and reactions, and express their ideas without excessive pressure of peer competition.

Inquiry-discovery teaching is an indirect teaching method. The teacher becomes a guide and facilitator to set students on the road to discovery. The teacher must supply information and materials as students need and inquire about task-relevant information. Inquiry learning involves manipulation of the learning environment in ways which are meaningful and relevant to students. A variety of well selected materials can serve to guide students towards the discovery of concepts and principles. Environments in which students are free to choose alternative instructional materials tend to increase inquiry activity.

The use of media is especially appropriate to the introduction of problems and the exploration of ideas and hypotheses which students formulate. Learning centers, for example, provide the necessary freedom of manipulation and availability of materials which inquiry learning requires. Small group instruction offers an excellent means of hypothesis testing and physical manipulation of materials, and role playing is a natural outlet for testing and manipulating social problems and questions.

In all situations, students should be actively and meaningfully involved in a personal learning situation. Children will sense problems, ask questions, request and gather information before making decisions when decisions are necessary but no specific problems demand solution. "Inquiry, in essence, is the pursuit of meaning by seeing if one's own ideas about an object, or phenomenon, are substantiated by one's actual experiences with, or observations of it (Strain, 1970, p. 117)."

Creativity is inherently related to the discovery process. Creativity is present in the production of questions and hypotheses, and in the combination of known facts and principles into manipulations of the unknown and development of solution strategies. Experience with discovery learning enhances creative performance by forcing the learner to manipulate the environment and produce new ideas.

The learner must be flexible to examine alternative solution strategies and hypotheses, and must elaborate and define needs in the quest for information. All of the creative processes, fluency, flexibility, elaboration, and originality are thus incorporated in the discovery-inquiry problem-solving process.

The basic considerations to be met in an inquiry learning experience are:

1. Provide the initial experience to interest students in inquiring about a problem, concept, situation, or idea. The use of media, role-playing, or puzzling demonstrations are generally successful investigative starters. Learning centers with a number of viable options provide an excellent beginning.
2. Provide the students with manipulative situations and materials to begin avenues of exploration. Games, media, files, sourcebooks, and discussions are all good starters.
3. Supply information sources for students' questions. Outside sources, field trips, speakers, peers, and the teacher are good supplements to written sources. The community and the world at large are fair game in the information seeking stage.
4. Provide materials and equipment that will spark and encourage student experimentation and production.
5. Provide time for students to manipulate, discuss, experiment, fail, and succeed.
6. Provide guidance, reassurance, and reinforcement for student ideas and hypotheses.
7. Reward and encourage acceptable solutions and solution strategies. Use failing experiences as instructional motivators. Have children question why a solution will not work and ask open-ended questions. A supportive positive climate will spawn the best results.

Expecting the Unexpected:
Questioning Techniques

In order to help children become good thinkers, we need to give them something to think about. The most common method of getting children to think is to ask questions. However, asking questions that require children to think requires much more thought and preparation by the teacher than asking questions which have one correct response. Convergent questions that have one right answer are useful in evaluating the learning of information, but they require few thinking skills on either the part of the teacher or the learner.

Questions which facilitate creative thinking are divergent or open-ended questions. These questions are often the springboard for a discussion because they have a number of possible answers. In his book *Creative Learning and Teaching* Torrance (1970) devotes four chapters to the questioning process. He especially advocates the use of provocative questions.

Open-ended questions are stimulating if the children express interest in the subject area, and they may evoke questions from the students as a consequence of the teacher's questioning. In order to be effective, open-ended questions must deal with material familiar to the students.

Divergent questions can provide access to all of the cognitive skills children need to acquire. Questions can be asked at all thinking levels and abilities. Higher level questions (analysis and evaluation) produce better evaluative skills than do the questions on lower levels. Questioning divergently helps children develop skills in gathering facts, formulating hypotheses, and testing their information.

Questioning also supplies valuable information to the teacher. Carin (1970) lists seven reasons teachers ask questions.

1. To arouse interest and motivate children to participate actively in a lesson.
2. To evaluate pupils' preparation and to see if their homework or previous work has been mastered.
3. To review and summarize what is taught.
4. To develop insights by helping children see new relationships.
5. To stimulate critical thinking and development of questioning attitudes.
6. To stimulate pupils to seek out additional knowledge on their own.
7. To evaluate the achievement of goals and objectives of lessons. (Carin, 1970, p. 14.)

Here are some guidelines to follow in developing your own questioning techniques:

1. Prepare questions before a lesson.
2. Ask questions simply and directly and avoid excessive wording. Vary the way you word questions. Ask Questions which stimulate students'

51

creative thinking processes (comparison, just suppose, interpretation, criticism, etc.).

3. Use some simple information questions to break the ice and to induce student participation, particularly for children who are fearful about responding to thought questions.

4. Allow sufficient time, after a question is asked, for children to think and to formulate possible answers or responses. Avoid calling on the first student whose hand is up.

5. Reinforce and encourage all children's efforts to respond even though their contributions might be wrong. If a child's response is incorrect, try to avoid any sense of ridicule or "put down". If possible try to help the child work through to a correct answer.

Here are some illustrative questions based on the concepts of fluency, flexibility , and originality for a lesson on the Pony Express (Feldhusen, 1983):

Fluency: What are all the ways mail might have been transported across the United States at that time?

Flexibility: Most of the time we think of the horse as a means of transportation for the rider and mail. Can you think of other ways a horse could have been used to communicate information from one place to another?

Originality: Can you think of some very unusual way that no one else has thought of to transport mail today?

Questions to induce higher level thinking can also be developed using Guilford's Structure of Intellect operations as a guide (Guilford, 1971). The operations are memory, cognition, divergent thinking, convergent thinking, and evaluation. Examples of questions at each level of operation are presented next.

Memory: Where did the battle take place?

Cognition: What did Sam mean when he said "They'll rue this day."

Divergent: What if the battle had never started? What would have been the course of events in Russia?

Convergent: How did social and economic factors combine to alter the course of the war?

Evaluation: In your opinion was the Vietnam war justified?

Memory questions call for simple recall of information. Cognition questions may call for comprehension or interpretation. Divergent questions call for creative speculation or for new ideas. Convergent questions pose a problem and ask for a solution. Evaluation questions ask for opinions, judgment or decisions based on values.

Questions to induce higher level thinking can also be based on the Bloom Taxonomy (1956). The six levels of the taxonomy are (1) knowledge,

(2) comprehension, (3) application, (4) analysis, (5) synthesis, and (6) judgment. Examples of questions at each level follow:

Knowledge: List the major causes of World War I as stated in Jones' text.

Comprehension: Explain the concept of détente and give illustration of détente in action.

Application: If the temperature rises and the amount of gas pressure increases, what would be the stress impact on the metal container?

Analysis: What are the major components of a book? Compare and contrast their importance to the reader.

Synthesis: Using the concepts of gerontology, describe an ideal pattern of behavior in old age.

Judgment: Using standards of literary criticism, critique Jone's essay on modern education.

Some of the examples are suggestions for discussion, not questions. However, all reflect techniques for interaction between teacher and students. The higher level questions in the Guilford model are divergent, convergent and evaluation. In the Bloom model they are application, analysis, synthesis, and judgment. With careful planning and practice teachers can develop higher level thinking skills with these higher level questions. Some questions at the lower levels will also be appropriate as a part of the total class discussion.

Critical Thinking

There is more to thinking than meets the ear. The ability to give the right answer to a question may or may not be a significant accomplishment, depending on the thought processes that took place before the answer surfaced. Critical thinking involves evaluation and consideration of the information available to the thinker. Critical thinking involves creative thinking because it requires the thinker to assimilate information and hypothesize solutions to problems.

Five basic steps are employed in the critical thinking process:

1. Recognizing problems.
2. Formulating hypotheses.
3. Gathering pertinent facts or data.
4. Testing and evaluation.
5. Drawing conclusions.

Classroom activities can be geared to developing critical thinking in students. Instruction must be organized in such a way that students are supplied background information and allowed to manipulate the information and discuss problems in order to discover their own conclusions. By learning to think critically, students learn to utilize and incorporate their acquired knowledge in a cumulative and productive manner.

Questioning and discussion sessions which employ divergent questioning techniques facilitate critical thinking. Students who are critical thinkers also need to be questioning learners. Situational learning which provides information but causes a student to seek information rather than to simply process given information will aid in the development of critical thinking. Learning by doing, role playing, solving cases and problems, and experimentation are situational learning experiences. Simulations are also excellent ways to actively involve students in a learning situation and to induce and teach critical thinking.

Critical thinking is the productive thinking ability that enables us to solve problems, plan and implement ideas and activities, and handle life without a floor plan or set of directions. It should be the most important phenomenon of learning for a teacher to develop, and it definitely is a creative, productive activity.

Ennis (1962), p. 84) offered 12 criteria of critical thinking:

1. Grasping the meaning of a statement.
2. Judging whether there is ambiguity in a line of reasoning.
3. Judging whether certain statements contradict each other.
4. Judging whether a conclusion follows necessarily.
5. Judging whether a statement is specific enough.
6. Judging whether a statement is actually the application of a certain principle.
7. Judging whether an observation statement is reliable.
8. Judging whether an inductive conclusion is warranted.
9. Judging whether the problem has been identified.
10. Judging whether something is an assumption.
11. Judging whether a definition is adequate.
12. Judging whether a statement made by an alleged authority is acceptable.

These criteria could be used as valuable guidelines to the teacher who is developing critical thinking activities in her classroom.

Two books from Midwest Publications (Harnadek, 1976, 1980), each titled *Critical Thinking* offer excellent experiences in the development of basic critical thinking skills. Students learn the basic skills of critical thinking and apply them to a variety of realistic situations and print media. These materials have been widely used in gifted programs and found to be effective in teaching critical thinking skills.

Brainstorming

Brainstorming is a technique used to produce ideas related to a particular problem, topic, or theme. It is an excellent technique for strengthening imagination, flexibility, and discussion techniques. It is also a highly successful tool for problem solving that can be conveniently used in nearly every subject area and situation.

All ideas should be recorded. If the "recorders" are writing ideas, two work better than one since the ideas sometimes come fast and heavy. A tape recorder is a good backup device to make sure no ideas are missed. It is also good to put all ideas on the blackboard because then they are available for all to see. Students can build on one another's ideas.

It is good to gather all participants into a circle if possible, but normal classroom seating in rows will also be acceptable. It is also desirable to give students experience in brainstorming in small groups of four to six students. Announce the topic well before the actual brainstorming session. When the session begins the topic should be restated and students should be told the ground rules:

1. Do not criticize or evaluate any ideas produced. Ideas should be free-flowing and unhampered at this stage.
2. Crazy or humorous ideas are acceptable. Wild imaginative ideas may become practical when forced into problem situations from a different viewpoint. The emergence of an unusual or bizarre idea may spark yet another idea.
3. Quantity of ideas is important. Quality of ideas is not considered at this point. The more ideas there are, the greater the base for evaluating and selecting viable ideas becomes.
4. Work with others in the combination of ideas. No one person's idea belong to that person; all ideas at this stage are thrown into the communal pot. Ideas that sprout from other ideas that have been suggested are fair game.

Participants should be allowed to express their ideas as they come, but one at a time so that all ideas are recorded. "Hitchhiking" is welcomed. That is, if one participant gets an idea from another's idea, he/she should be allowed to give the new response immediately. Combining two or more responses is acceptable and encouraged. Students should also be taught to be brief or succinct in contributing ideas in brainstorming and to avoid discussion of ideas during brainstorming sessions.

The secret to brainstorming is deferred judgment. This means that criticism is ruled out. All responses are accepted and evaluation (good or bad) is withheld until later. Some teachers like to keep a bell or buzzer handy to use as a warning signal that someone is criticizing or evaluating. Freewheeling is also welcomed. Wild, bizarre ideas are welcomed. Students can also leapfrog or build on one another's ideas.

In brainstorming, the emphasis should be on quantity. Quality implies evaluation, which comes after the brainstorming session. Quantity is important. The larger the number of ideas produced, the more likely that many of them will be useful ones. The ideas generated tend to get more original as the session continues. Common ideas will be generated at first, then participants begin to stretch their minds for unusual responses as the less obvious responses are offered.

After the session is over, members should be provided with a typed copy listing all the ideas generated. This can be used for further exploration, combination of ideas, and final selection of potentially useful ideas. Evaluation and selection of ideas to be implemented or developed should come from each member or from a select committee *after* the brainstorming session. It is often a good idea to have a postsession request for late ideas and thoughts. Then students can be assigned to project work groups to plan, elaborate, develop, and implement the ideas.

The topic for brainstorming should cover the problem statement but be broad enough to allow for freedom of thought. For example, when brainstorming for a unit on the family in social studies class, the question might be, "What are all the ways families could increase cohesiveness and togetherness?" For a unit on Japan, the question might be, "What are all the things we would like to learn about Japan?" In both instances, the ideas generated would be used as the foundations for developing other learning activities.

Brainstorming can be used in almost any area of the curriculum. Students can also be given problems in classroom planning and management (how to solve a discipline problem, things to be done in planning for a forthcoming field trip). In all instances brainstorming sessions should be followed by an evaluation session in which the best or most promising ideas are identified and plans are made for individuals or small groups to work on developing, elaborating, and implementing them.

Attribute Listing

The combination or modification of old ideas, concepts, and principles into new and novel ones is the basic premise behind creative thinking. Attribute listing is a technique that promotes a clearer view of the qualities, specifications, characteristics, limitations, and attributes of a problem to allow for easy change and the development of new ideas through the change.

Paper and pencil, chalkboard, transparency material, and an overhead projector are the main items of equipment needed. Attribute listing can be done by individual children or combined with informal brainstorming in group work.

The teacher can begin an attribute listing group project by defining the problem and writing it where it is readily visible to all the children. Then a chart such as appears in Figure 4.1 should be developed. In column form, three lists should be developed. In the first column, the problem is broken down into parts or components. In column two, the characteristics or attributes of each part are listed. In column three, ideas for improvement, based

Part or Component	Characteristics or Attribute	Ideas for Improvement
1. The ground surface	1. Grass Blacktop Concrete	1. Need more grass Use artificial turf
2. The placement of play equipment	2. In rows Close together	2. Vary placement Spread out Make game area
3. The baseball diamond	3. At far corner On dirt area	3. Put in grass Stationary bases
4. The swings	4. Very tall Metal chain Wooden seats	4. Need small ones Belt seats better
5. The water fountains	5. One fountain Made of concrete	5. Need more fountains Needs steps
6. The fence around it	6. Very high Chain link Blocks vision	6. Make it lower More open

Figure 4.1. Problem: How to improve the playground

on ideas generated in columns one and two, are written. Some teachers supply handouts with column one already filled in.

After the ideas have been developed and listed they can be easily examined, discussed, and elaborated upon. If they pass evaluation and receive approval from the group, the final step is implementation and resulting modification or solution of the problem.

Attribute listing can be used as a springboard for stimulating class discussions. The possibilities are endless. Social studies discussions, discussions of scientific principles and problems, character studies and story writing and discussions, and problem solving are some suggested areas in which attribute listing can be used.

Attribute listing can take place in large class discussions, in small group work, or individually. Attribute listing is a useful technique for developing new ideas. It is an excellent method for teaching the cognitive skills of analysis, fluency, flexibility, evaluation and elaboration.

Morphological Analysis

The technique of morphological analysis involves studying two or more components of a problem. Whereas attribute listing or "check-list" techniques

	Components				
Materials	Floors	Walls	Desks	Tables	Chalk-boards
Paper	Paper footprints to guide movement	Murals for walls	Paper desk pads for scratch paper work		
Cardboard	Use large pieces of cardboard as room dividers	Partitions study carrells	Use Tri-wall cardboard to build desks	Put cardboard boxes on tables for storage	Could get more black boards by painting black on cardboard
Felt/Cloth	Bring in scraps to sew together to make a classroom carpet	Put up felt/burlap strips for display purposes	Make cushions for desk chairs		
Paint		May not be possible to do in some schools	Let each child decorate desk	Have color-coded tables for learning stations	Slate paint on walls, ceiling boards
Rubber	Old tires for sitting in				
Glass		Partitions to cut sound and noise down		Glass tops to lay over desks and tables with instructions underneath	
Plastic		Egg carton wall partitions good acoustic devices			

Figure 4.2. Problem: Improving the classroom environment using common materials and available equipment

focus on modification principles, morphological analysis focuses on the principle of combinations. In morphological analysis we try to combine existing data or parts of a problem in new ways, to discover original ideas or solutions.

Morphological analysis usually employs a grid or matrix to help us study the problem and develop as many combinations as possible in a systematic manner.

Parameters. We begin by identifying the basic dimensions or components of the problem, which are called *parameters*. Although any problem might be analyzed using a large number of parameters, it is usually easiest if you try to identify from *two* to *five* basic components. For illustrations, problems can most easily be represented by two or three parameters (which can be drawn as a square or a cube).

For example, in Figure 4.2, we have considered the problem, "How might we improve the classroom environment using common materials and available equipment?" In this example, there are two parameters: *components of the classroom,* and *available materials.*

A second example involves the problem, "What are some effective ways of creating program options for gifted students?" This problem, illustrated in Figure 4.3, has been analyzed using four parameters: *people* who might work with gifted students, *places* where learning might occur in unique ways, *processes to be encouraged, and products* which might result.

Attributes. After listing the parameters of the problem, the next step is to list the *attributes* for each parameter. For example, the components of the classroom in Figure 4.2 (which are attributes) were: floors, walls, desks, tables, and chalkboards. The attributes of the other parameter, materials, were: paper, cardboard, felt-cloth, etc.

Once the attributes are listed, the next step is to *test all the possible combinations.* Try to find ways to combine each attribute of the first parameter with each of the attributes of the other parameters, to try to identify new combinations or original ideas. Not *every* combination will be productive, of course (in Figure 4.3, there are 50,625 possible combinations). However, it is quite likely that you will discover some new, unusual, and valuable ideas.

Morphological analysis is a formal way of bringing ideas together into new possibilities and unusual combinations. It requires clear explanations from the teacher concerning what is expected from the students and how to accomplish it. Treffinger (1979) proposed six steps:

1. Selecting partners
2. Listing attributes for each parameter
3. Developing evaluation ciriteria
4. Examining many combinations
5. Checking up on other resources
6. Following up on promising ideas

PEOPLE	PLACES	PROCESSES	PRODUCTS
Gifted Students	School	Basic Facts/ Information	Written Prose
Parents	Homes	Divergent Thinking	Solution—Action Plan
Teachers	Camps	Exploratory Experiences	Poems
Principals	Retreat/ Conference Ctr.	Problem Solving Steps	Songs/Music
Business People	Stores/Malls	Critical Thinking/Eval.	Visual/Artistic Media
Younger Children	Community Centers	"Higher Levels" (Applic/Anal/ Synthesis)	Story in News- papers
Older Children	Service Clubs	Research/Inquiry Methods	TV or Radio Program
School Board Members	Van or Mobile Center	Values Clarification	Movie, Slide, or Photo Story
Politician	Hotels/Motels	Independent Investigations	Dramatic Presentations
Civic Leaders	Parks, Zoo	Risk-Taking	Legislation
Retired/Sr. Citizens	Farms	Intuition	Construction/ Demolition
Counselor/ School Psyc.	Office Bldgs.	Complexity/ Challenge	Changing Commun. Attitudes
College Students	Corridors/Display Cases/Walls	Self-concept	Inventions/ Patents/Copyright
Scientists	Bus	Predicting Estimating	Videotape/audio
Professionals	Laboratories	Explaining	Monuments

Reprinted from G/C/T January-February, 1979, page 51.

Figure 4.3. Designing programs for the gifted and talented. Application of the morphological model.

If problems are selected that are really interesting or important to the students, substantial motivation and interest will be generated. Morphological analysis, when carried out well, can lead to significant and useful solutions. Above all, the students learn a successful technique for thinking and solving problems.

Synectics

If I were an idea, how would I like to be formulated? Many people have played such imagination games. The name of the game is synectics, and it was developed by William J. J. Gordon (Gordon, 1961). Synectics is a creative thinking technique that utilizes analogies and metaphors to help the thinker analyze problems and form different viewpoints. No equipment is necessary, but it is a good idea to have paper or a chalkboard handy to record ideas. The first step is to define the problem and to state it on the chalkboard for all to see. Work then proceeds with the class as a whole led by the teacher or in small groups led by students.

There are three types of analogies popular for use in synectics: (1) fantasy, (2) direct, and (3) personal. The use of fantasy analogy is the most common and is usually the lead-off in a synectics session. In fantasy analogies students search for the ideal solutions to a problem, but their solutions can be as far-fetched or unusual as possible. Solutions may be dreamed up in fanciful, whimsical, even animated dimensions. The teacher may start off a session by asking the students to think up the ideal solution for a problem involving movement of a heavy piece of equipment on the playground. Analogies may be fantasized that include tiny nymphlike creatures carrying the equipment skyward, use of elephants, or giant balloons. As in brainstorming all ideas are accepted, no ideas are criticized, and students can build on one another's fantasies. After generating a number of fantasy ideas, the teacher leads the class back to a practical evaluation and analysis of the ideas to determine which ones might be practically developed.

Another popular form of analogy is the direct analogy. Using this technique, students are asked to find parallel problem situations in real life situations. The problem might be how to move some heavy furniture in the classroom. The problem might be paralleled in real life situations by animals transporting their young. Spaceships carrying space exploration equipment would also be an example of the same problem situation in another setting. The main difference between fantasy and direct analogy procedures is that fantasy analogies can be entirely fictitious, whereas direct analogies must be actual parallels in real life to the problem. Again, all ideas are accepted, and the class tries later to examine the ideas for practical development.

Personal analogies require students to place themselves in the role of the problem itself. They might begin by saying "If I were a heavy swing set on the playground and I wanted to move to another place on the playground, what could I do? Well, I would reach up and pull down a big tree branch. Then I would release it and it would swing me to where I want to go."

The following narrative is illustrative of a synectics session. A fourth grade class is studying the organization of the post office. They have learned that breakage and damage is a major problem in the post office. The problem is written on the board as follows: How can heavy objects in the post office be moved with a minimum of manpower and maximum protection of the packages against damage? The class is taken on a field trip to the post office where they are told about the problems of package handling by postal workers.

After the return to the classroom, each student is asked to rewrite the problem on the board. Then the class identifies obvious solutions to the problem and writes them on the blackboard. Next, synectics discussion groups are organized. Each group must be led by the teacher or aides at the beginning of synectics training. Later, as they develop skill in synectics, students can lead their own sessions.

The leader begins with a fantasy analogy approach. Students are asked to imagine a situation in which packages are being moved. After a period of discussion, one student volunteers that the packages sprout arms and legs, and eyes and ears. The leader then asks for a forced combination of this analogy into the problem situation. The solution is then reexamined and it is suggested that the packages be placed on individual carrying devices that have remote sensing equipment and are self-propelled to a preprogrammed area.

Now, the leader asks for direct analogies. "What things move under their own direction and carry a heavy load?" Animals named are opossums and camels. A forced solution is then asked for between these animals and the problem at hand. Students hypothesize a device that is operated by pulleys and runs overhead, carrying packages suspended by hooks or magnets. This idea came from the analogy of opossums, which carry their babies clinging to their bellies. The idea of camels carrying weight between their humps is converted to mechanized carts with a large enclosed motor at each end, a carrying space between the motors, and a radar control system which directs the cart to a specified destination.

Finally, the leader asks for personal analogies. Students are assigned the role of packages and asked how they would like to be moved. The answers indicate concern for careful handling. One student shares a desire to float through the post office and settle gently at a destination. Another student asks to be moved with tender loving care. Forcing these ideas into the problem situation suggests that packages be allowed to float in a conveyor tank filled with foam packing pellets to appropriate stations in the post office.

At the end of the synectics sessions the leader summarizes the results and they are recorded on the board. In a follow up session the ideas are reviewed and evaluated, and the class finishes the activity by writing recommendations for package handling improvement to the Postmaster General or to the local postmaster.

Synectics is a stimulating way to involve students in imaginative discussions and come up with unusual and workable problem strategies. Any subject-related topic can be examined in small or large group discussions. Giving students an explanation of the method to be used and examples will help stimulate an effective synectics session. Through synectics students can learn valuable strategies for solving problems.

The synectics approach has been utilized in many powerful problem solving programs for business and industry, and in recent years, it has also begun to receive more attention in educational settings. Gordon and Poze (1975) developed some very useful materials, for example, in their *Making It Strange* series. These books provide excellent examples of methods and techniques that students can learn to help them use metaphor and analogy in "making new connections" for creative thinking and problem solving. Gordon and Poze (1980) have also demonstrated very effectively how the SES Synectics approach can be successfully used in heterogeneous classrooms. While the slower students used direct analogies, personal analogies, and compressed conflict statements to reinforce their comprehension of basic concepts, the same metaphoric strategies or "tools" were used by gifted students as "springboards" for more complex ideas and for richer, more detailed analyses of problems and topics.

Forced Relationships

The technique of forcing relationships is an associative thinking activity which helps develop the ability to see unusual uses for things and the combination of ideas from different viewpoints. The technique has four major approaches which will be summarized below. These are listing techniques, catalog techniques, focused relationships, and arbitrary forced relationships.

Listing Techniques. In this technique the problem statement is presented to the students. A list of unrelated objects is then presented, or generated by the teacher or children. This list has no relationship to the problem stated, and may in fact be produced before the introduction of the problem in order to lessen the tendency to choose related objects. The children must take each object on the list in turn and associate it with the problem statement. The objects themselves do not need to be related. The relationship should be derived by a free association method, that is, taking the first relationship that comes to mind. By doing this, judgment of the relationship is initially deferred. After all relationships have been recorded, the students go back through the list and evaluate the ideas for possible modification, development, and implementation. Evaluation of the responses should be recorded with a + or −. A third run through the responses serves as a planning stage to begin development of the ideas.

Here is an example of a forced relationship technique used to deal with the problem "Fighting on the Playground."

List	Freely Associated Responses	Evaluation
magazine	Take magazines to playground for diversion of fighters.	+
grass	If they must fight, grass is better than blacktop, so plant grass.	+
oil	Oil shoes of the fighters so they can't stand up.	−
shoe	Make the fighters go barefoot in warm weather. Blacktop and gravel will hurt feet and prevent fighting.	−
puzzles	Give children puzzles to solve to calm them down.	+
ice	Use ice cream to reward good behavior.	+
typewriter	Let children type to reward good behavior.	+

Catalog Techniques. This technique is much like the listing technique. The problem is stated first. However, objects to be used in association with problem solutions are drawn randomly from a catalog. The catalog is opened at random and the student can use any object as seen there in creating a solution. The objects are then forced to fit the problem statement. The same steps of evaluation, development, and implementation are then followed as in listing.

Focused Relationships. Focussing relationships follow the same line as the catalog or listing techniques. However, the relationship of the objects to the problem statement is not completely random or arbitrary. The objects which will be forced to the problem statement should be preselected and in some way be relevant to the problem. For example, in the problem "Fighting on the Playground," typewriter would not be selected as a forceable object, but grass and shoe might be. Playground equipment, boxing gloves, rocks, and blacktop would be relevant to the problem. As with the other technique, the relationship of the objects to the problem is freely associated, one object at a time. Evaluation is held off until all of the relationships have been created. Then development and implementation of the ideas are undertaken.

Arbitrary Forced Relationships. Arbitrary forced relationships do not involve the use of a problem statement. All that is needed is a group of arbitrary words, objects, or ideas. Two objects are selected at random and forced together. Ideas that are produced using this technique can then be developed. One good method of presentation is to fill a fish bowl with objects written on folded slips of paper. The thinker must pull out two slips, read the names of the objects, and force them together to create a novel idea.

Classroom Strategies. These forced relationship techniques can be stimulating activities for the whole class, or very productive activities for individual students. They can be easily adapted for use in learning centers, and for seatwork activities between longer activities during the day. Here are some suggestions for using forced relationships techniques in classroom situations:

1. Provide catalogs for students to draw objects from and a list of problems from which students may pick those which they find interesting or stimulating.
2. Use a fishbowl or an idea box in a corner of the room or make a bulletin board with an idea box. Display students' ideas and forced relationships.
3. Provide words in lists for students to associate with a problem. Have a competition between two groups of students using the same lists and two different problems.
4. Let students brainstorm relevant ideas and objects for a particular problem, and then force relationships between their list and the problem.

These techniques can be used in almost any problems situation, whether it is subject matter related, or related to other classroom activities. They provide excellent experience in associative thinking and help children become better creative thinkers and problem solvers.

Creative Problem Solving

Several models of problem solving have been developed under the rubric of creative problem solving. Generally these models do not involve single answer or single solution problems. Rather they focus on problems for which many different solutions may be feasible. All these models also give the student some opportunity to participate in the problem identification and clarification process. Finally the creative problem solving model is generally used with realistic, practical problems whereas single solution problems frequently focus on puzzles or unreal and impractical problems.

Torrance and Myers (1970) presented one widely used model in their book *Creative Learning and Teaching* (p. 78). The model involves five steps or stages. Torrance and Myers urged that attention first be paid to establishing facilitative conditions prior to attempting to solve actual problems. Students' basic creative abilities and attitudes can then be developed with many excellent training programs currently on the market. There should also be a period of "warm up" and an effort to establish a supportive climate in which there is

65

freedom to express ideas openly and stimulation to pursue good ideas. The steps in the Torrance and Myers model are:

1. Sensing problems and challenges
2. Recognizing the real problem
3. Producing alternative solutions
4. Evaluating ideas
5. Preparing to put ideas into use

Students can work individually or in small groups with some pacing and guidance from the teacher. The third step can involve any of the other creative thinking strategies we have discussed in this book such as brainstorming, synectics, attribute listing or forced choices.

The work of Alex Osborn (1963) led to many other developments in defining and teaching Creative Problem Solving (e.g., Parnes, 1967; Parnes, Noller, & Biondi, 1977; Isaksen & Treffinger, 1985). This approach involves a multi-stage model, described as "CPS," in which the stages are:

1. Mess-Finding
2. Data-Finding
3. Problem-Finding
4. Idea-Finding
5. Solution-Finding
6. Acceptance-Finding

General objectives for CPS are given in Figure 4.4.

Mess-Finding involves considering your goals and concerns and your own personal orientation or "style" of dealing with problems, in order to determine the most important or immediate starting point for your problem solving efforts. In Mess-Finding, your major concern is to determine a broad goal or area of concern towards which your CPS efforts will be directed.

Data-Finding involves examining all of the information and impressions available about the "Mess." In this stage, you will be "sifting through" all of the data surrounding your Mess—the facts, the feelings, the questions, and the hunches and concerns that you feel—to help you to understand the "Mess" better. In Data-Finding, you are attempting to clarify the most important directions you should follow during the subsequent CPS steps.

Problem-Finding. In this stage, your major task is to take the most important information that you located in the previous stage, and begin to formulate specific problem statements; you are defining the problem. In any Mess on which you're working, there may be many different problems that *might* be solved; in Problem-Finding, we are trying to state as many different problems or sub-problems as possible, so we can better select an appropriate problem on which to work.

1. **Be sensitive to problems***

    Given a "mess" the student should be able to describe many specific problems which could be appropriately attacked;

    Describe many elements of a situation;

    Employ a checklist to extend analysis of possible problems

2. **Be able to define problems**

    Given a perplexing situation, the student should be able to:

    —recognize the "hidden" or "real" problem which may underlie the stated question;

    —broaden the problem, or redefine it by asking "why";

    —redefine or clarify the problem by changing verbs;

    —identify several possible sub-problems

3. **Be able to break away from habit-bound thinking**

    Given a description of a common situation, the student should be able to:

    —describe habitual ways of responding;

    —evaluate the effectiveness of those responses;

    —develop several possible alternative ways of responding;

    —select promising alternatives;

    —develop and implement a plan for using new responses

4. **Be able to defer judgment**

    In viewing a perplexing situation, be able to:

    —produce many responses;

    —give responses without imposing evaluations;

    —refrain from evaluating others' responses.

5. **Be able to see new relationships**

    Given perplexing situations or stimuli, be able to:

    —identify similarities among objects or experiences;

    —identify differences among objects or experiences;

    —list ideas for relating or comparing objects/experiences

6. **Be able to evaluate the consequences of one's actions**

    Identify a variety of criteria for evaluation;

    Develop many possible criteria for any problem;

    Demonstrate deferred judgment with respect to criteria

---

*Reprinted from Treffinger & Huber (1975).

Figure 4.4. Specific objectives for creative problem solving

Idea-Finding. Once you have formulated an appropriate and workable problem statement, the next step is to generate as many ideas as possible. You are trying to generate or produce as many possible solutions as you can for the problem. During this stage, you may use many different techniques or strategies for producing new and unusual ideas. The principle of *deferred judgment* (Osborn, 1963) is very important to remember. Since you are attempting to find as many solution ideas as possible, evaluating too soon or too much may inhibit your thinking and cause you to overlook very unusual or promising ideas. It's much easier to go back later and evaluate your ideas than it is to try to retrieve one really imaginative idea that was lost or held back by evaluation.

Solution-Finding. After a list of ideas has been developed, you will want to determine which ones are the most promising solutions for the problem. Solution-Finding helps you to do this. In this stage, you will first generate possible criteria to use in evaluating the ideas on your list; then, you will use those criteria to conduct a detailed and systematic evaluation of the ideas. You are not simply trying to select one idea and eliminate all the rest, nor are you looking only for "perfect" ideas. You are attempting to locate, from among all the ideas you have generated, the ones that you believe have the greatest potential for solving the problem.

Acceptance-Finding. A good idea is not worth much unless it is put to use. In Acceptance-Finding, you will take the promising ideas that you identified in Solution-Finding, and decide how they can best be implemented. What help will you need? What obstacles might need to be overcome? What specific steps will need to occur? Acceptance-Finding is primarily concerned with helping *good* ideas become *useful* ideas.

This creative problem solving model has been widely used and evaluated with older students and adults and found to be readily learned and used (Torrance, 1972; Reese, Parnes, Treffinger & Kaltsounis, 1976). Specific objectives for creative problem solving were described by Treffinger and Huber (1975). This comprehensive list is presented in Figure 4.4.

Noller (1977) developed a shortened and simplified explanation of the CPS model in her small book, Scratching the Surface of Creative Problem Solving: A Bird's Eye-View of CPS. She stressed that the term "finding" which is hyphenated in each step accents the hunting, searching for ideas which characterizes CPS. She also noted that problems usually begin with a mess because everything is ill defined and poorly understood. Steps one and two move the problems solver to a clear conception of the problem as a prelude and guide to finding ideas and solutions. Parnes (1977) has also provided guidelines for using the CPS material with gifted students, and Noller, Treffinger, and Houseman (1979) have provided a short book which can be used to illustrate applications of CPS in gifted education. Parnes (1981) provided an informal but thorough discussion of the five-step CPS approach, and included many examples of useful activities and exercises to assist students in learning the process. In addition, Parnes' extensive use of cartoons provides an effective and informal overview of many important concepts that can be very useful with adults as well as children. Treffinger, Isaksen, and Firestien (1982) have also provided advanced resources, methods, and techniques that are useful in applying CPS in instructional settings. Firestien & Treffinger (1983) also offered practical guidelines for classroom applications of CPS, with particular emphasis on ways to use CPS in independent study. Isaksen & Treffinger (1985) have developed an updated and expanded instructional program that provides a very comprehensive presentation of CPS methods and activities.

The first author of this book has developed and used two models of creative problem solving which he has found to be highly effective in teaching students the processes of CPS. The first model, illustrated in Figure 4.5, borrows from the models described above but is unique in several respects. In stage one students work in small groups and identify their own problem but within a curricular framework specified by the teacher. In the illustration in Figure 4.5 the framework is the energy crisis, possibly a social studies problem. Brainstorming is used to identify problems, and the evaluation process is used to select out first three, then one, most critical problems.

Stage two is a clarification process. Students are urged to discuss the problem by giving illustrations of it, speculating about causes and so forth. Stage three is then a problem specifying process. Here the problem is written in as precise language as possible, and students are taught some appropriate forms for problem statements.

Stage four involves generating ideas using all the good creative thinking techniques such as synectics and attribute analysis. Then in stage five students synthesize their ideas into a single composite solution which utilizes as many of their stage four ideas as possible. They also test the fit of their solution to the problem statement.

Finally in stage six students learn how to plan for implementation of their solution. How will the solution be put to use? Who will do it? What sequence of events will be followed? etc.

With practice students can become fluent in using the model for a wide variety of problems in English, social studies, science and career education.

The second CPS model developed by Feldhusen, is called "A Simplified CPS Model" and is illustrated in Figure 4.6. It has been used extensively with elementary school children. It is very similar to the model discussed above, but it places less emphasis on precise problem clarification and identification. In this model there is also less emphasis on curriculum problems. Children get experience in identifying and solving problems which are a part of their daily lives.

These creative problem solving models provide excellent opportunities for students to engage actively in the thinking skills illustrated in the left margin of Figure 4.5. They also learn a valuable and comprehensive strategy for dealing with personal and curriculum problems. Evaluation by the first author of this book of a large number of students and teachers who have worked with these CPS models indicates that they provide experiences which are enjoyable and educationally valuable (Feldhusen & Moore, 1979).

Processes		
	I.	**Problem Generation**
		A. What are some problems our country faces as a result
Fluency		of the energy crisis?
Flexibility		
Originality		Brainstorm problem identification.
Deferred		
Judgment		
Evaluation		B. What are the most critical and general problems? Pick
		3, then 1
	II.	**Problem Clarification**
		A. What are illustrations of the problem?
Analysis		B. What are things that *cause* the problem?
Evaluation		C. What are further problems caused by the problem?
		D. What are attributes, characteristics or dimensions of
		the problem?
	III.	**Problem Identification**
Synthesis		A. State the problem in light of stage II discussion as
		precisely as possible.
	IV.	**Idea Finding**
		A. Brainstorm for solutions
Fluency		1. What could we do?
Flexibility		2. What could be changed?
Analysis		B. Forced association
Originality		C. Attribute analysis
Deferred		D. Synectics
Judgment		E. Solving parts of the problem
	V.	**Synthesizing a Solution**
Synthesis		A. Pick out the best elements from stage IV.
Elaboration		B. Develop a Gestalt-closure
Evaluation		C. Does it fit to the problem statement?
	VI.	**Implementation**
		A. Who will do what?
Synthesis		B. How will it be done?
Evaluation		C. What temporal sequence will be followed?
Originality		D. What precautions and obstacles must be watched for?
Flexibility		E. Locations?
		F. How to overcome obstacles?

Figure 4.5. Example of creative problem solving

1. Begin by having children brainstorm in small groups problems they have on the playground. Remind them of rules:

   (a) someone records all ideas
   (b) everyone must contribute
   (c) state ideas briefly
   (d) there is to be *no* criticism, discussion or evaluation
   (e) quantity is a goal
   (f) they can build on one another's ideas
   (g) funny ideas are acceptable

2. In phase two the group evaluates the list, discusses the problem, selects the three most serious or important, then the one most important.

3. In phase three the children brainstorm solutions to *the* problem. Follow same rules as above. Solutions can be full or partial ways of solving the problem.

4. In phase four they take ideas presented in phase three and create a synthesis for a solution. The solution might be eclectic, but it should hang together.

5. Develop a plan for implementing the solution. Who, where, when, how? Write the plan and turn it in.

Figure 4.6. Example of a simplified CPS model

Torrance and others (Torrance, 1978; Torrance, Bruch and Torrance, 1976) have also utilized creative problem-solving processes and procedures in developing an extensive program in *future problem solving*. Students from many school districts throughout the United States have learned how to use creative problem-solving procedures to deal with problems concerning the future. Students from both elementary and secondary schools have participated in "Future Problem Solving Bowl" programs, which have been conducted for several years in Athens, Georgia (at the University of Georgia) and in Lincoln, Nebraska (at the University of Nebraska). The national headquarters of the Future Problem Solving Program is now St. Andrews College, Laurenburg, North Carolina 28352.

Another national program that has helped many students learn how to apply creative thinking and problem solving methods in realistic settings is the *Odyssey of the Mind* program. In this program, teams of students at various age levels create original solutions to a variety of "design" or construction-type problems. Although it is possible for teams to compete at a variety of levels, and to have their ideas judged on a number of different criteria, we believe that the important contribution of such a program is to give students an opportunity to put creative thinking and problem solving to work in dealing with unusual and appealing problems; competitive aspects should not be allowed to become the dominant goals. For additional information, contact Creative Competitions, Inc., Glassboro, NJ 08028.

Measuring Creativity

Few topics in the area of creativity and gifted education have been more controversial and perplexing than that of measuring creativity. One of the major questions that should be considered, of course, is one's *purpose* for measuring creativity in the first place. We believe that there is little justification for using tests of creativity for labeling students or for selecting a "fixed" group of students for a general program for "gifted" students. We do not believe that constructive educational purposes are served by using creative test scores to establish rigid "cutoff" scores for identification, nor to determine specific formulas or minimum requirements for "eligibility" for specific programs.

Creative measures may be useful for educators, however, for other reasons. First, they may help us to identify certain learning characteristics of students that might otherwise go unrecognized. Creativity measurement data may help to remind us that we should seek and value students who can think of many possibilities, who can readily look at problems from many points of view, or who can develop unusual or original ideas. Second, creativity measures may give us information that can be useful to us in designing stimulating and effective ways of individualizing instructional planning. Information about students' creative thinking abilities may guide us in planning appropriate and challenging instructional activities for them. Third, creativity measurement data can be useful in helping us evaluate the effectiveness of instructional programs that are intended to nurture skills related to independent, creative learning and problem solving.

For these purposes, we believe that educators should not rely on a single source of information or an overall, composite score or index. It is much more appropriate, in our view, to utilize multiple data sources (scores, ratings, observations, and product evaluation) to obtain a *profile* of information about the student's creative thinking abilities and accomplishments.

There are many creativity instruments, checklists, and rating scales that can provide useful information when properly administered, scored, and interpreted. We have provided a brief bibliography of some of the most commonly-used resources. For more detailed information, you should consult a standard reference source, such as the Buros *Mental Measurements Yearbooks,* as well as the specific technical manuals that accompany test instruments.

Summary

These various methods and techniques for teaching creative thinking, problem solving, inquiry, and critical thinking can be incorporated into the regular classroom subject matter or they can be organized as separate experiences for gifted programs. If they are related to subject matter, they will enhance both subject matter learning and the acquisition of skills in creative thinking and problem solving. It is important to remember that in using any of these methods, the goal is not to solve problems as such. Rather it is to help students develop their abilities to solve many kinds of problems in and out of school.

SOME POPULAR INSTRUMENTS FOR ASSESSING VARIOUS ASPECTS OF CREATIVE ABILITY

Feldhusen, J. F. *Creativity Self Rating Scale.* Gifted Education Resource Institute, Purdue University, West Lafayette, Indiana 47906.

Feldhusen, J. F. and others. *Purdue Elementary Problem Solving Inventory.* Gifted Education Resource Institute, Purdue University, West Lafayette, Indiana 47906.

Guilford, J. P. and others. *Creativity Tests for Children.* Sheridan Psychological Services, P.O. Box 6101, Orange, California 92667.

Khatena, S., and Torrance, E. P. *Khatena-Torrance Creative Perception Inventory.* The Stoelting Company, 1350 S. Kostner Avenue, Chicago, Illinois 60623.

Meeker, M. *A Rating Scale for Identifying Creative Potential.* SOI Institute, 214 Main Street, El Segundo, California, 90245.

Renzulli, J. S. and others, *Scales for Rating Behavioral Characteristics of Superior Students.* Creative Learning Press, P.O. Box 320, Mansfield Center, Connecticut, 06250.

Rimm, S. B. *Group Inventory for Finding Creative Talent.* Educational Assessment Service, Route One, Watertown, Wisconsin, 53094.

Ross, J. D. and Ross, C. M. *Ross Tests of Higher Cognitive Processes.* Academic Therapy Publications, P.O. Box 899, 1539 Fourth Street, San Rafael, California, 94901.

Taylor, C. W. and others. *Alpha Biographical Inventory.* Institute for Behavioral Research on Creativity, University of Utah, Salt Lake City, Utah, 84100.

Torrance, E. P., Khatena, J. and Cunnington, B. F. *Thinking Creatively With Sounds and Words.* Scholastic Testing Service, 480 Meyer Road, Bensenville, Illinois 60106.

Torrance, E. P. *Torrance Tests of Creative Thinking.* Scholastic Testing Service, 480 Meyer Road, Bensenville, Illinois 60106.

Chapter 5

HOW TO GET A PROJECT STARTED
IN YOUR CLASSROOM

By now, you are probably ready to get started using some of these new ideas in your classroom. Even if you have already been doing some of these things (and we know that many good teachers are already using them!) we hope that you have found some interesting new techniques. The purpose of this chapter is to give you some practical suggestions about how to get started in an organized, exciting program to develop creative thinking and problem solving among your gifted and talented students.

Six General Guidelines

Your efforts at helping gifted children become better creative thinkers and problem solvers will be successful and more rewarding for you and your students if you approach your goal very systematically. There are six general guidelines which will help in planning, conducting, and evaluating your classroom project. They are:

1. Know how to define creative thinking and problem-solving processes and abilities.
2. Be explicit in specifying the processes, skills, and content you will help the students in your class to learn and develop.
3. Try out your plans and new ideas before you begin to use them with your class.
4. Create an atmosphere in your class in which creative learning can occur.
5. Utilize learning procedures involving many activities and products.
6. Conduct a careful review and evaluation, not only of the students' learning, but of your own project and efforts, and plan revisions accordingly.

In this chapter, each of these guidelines will be discussed more specifically. We shall also point out some hazards and pitfalls you must be prepared to deal with during your project. We shall also offer some suggestions about opportunities for you to locate demonstration projects, and displays of useful resources and material are provided.

1. *Know how to define creative-thinking and problem-solving processes and abilities.*

At the very beginning, of course, *you* must be certain that you are clear and confident in your own understanding of creative thinking and problem solving. These are very complex processes of thinking and learning, and it is very important for you to maintain a "sharp image" of your goals!

What are some of the basic creative-thinking abilities with which you should be concerned? There are several basic thinking abilities; each of them contributes to the creative problem-solving process, and can be encouraged in your daily instruction. Creative-thinking abilities have also been the focus of the attention of many writers and program developers. Indeed, many of the instructional materials and programs that we have reviewed in this book emphasize the development of such abilities. In defining creative-thinking abilities, it is common to emphasize four basic abilities that involve divergent thinking (Guilford, 1967; Torrance, 1962, 1966). These are fluency, flexibility, originality, and elaboration.

Fluency is thinking of many possible ideas or responses; it is partially a memory process. An individual gathers and stores information until it can be of use. Fluency is then a selection retrieval process in which the individual sees the connection of stored information to an immediate problem (Davidson & Sternberg, 1984). Fluency can be observed in a class discussion when a pupil offers many ideas on one topic, or produces several ideas for the implementation of another individual's idea. Fluency is an important aspect of any idea generating component. A student who provides many responses in an idea producing session is illustrating fluency in thinking.

Flexibility is the ability to switch from one train of thought to another or to look at a problem in a new and different way. In problem solving and creativity, we must be able to look for a wide variety of applications or new kinds of ideas. Flexibility requires that we adapt to alternatives and find new situations and ideas. It also means not getting "locked into" rigid ways of viewing the problem. Flexible thinkers can use information in a variety of ways and produce ideas that are categorically different from one another. Flexibility can be observed in a class discussion when a pupil switches easily from one topic to another and incorporates several alternatives to each problem presented. A student who gets stuck on one idea, or who cannot relate his/her ideas to other pupils' ideas, is not being flexible.

Originality is the ability to produce novel, unique, or unusual ideas. Unusual ideas are the combination of two old ideas in a new dimension. It is often an association process of *seeing* connections between ideas that have never been linked before. The invention of the water bed may have originated in someone's desire to float off to sleep. Originality can be strengthened in students, by practice, acceptance of unusual ideas, and encouragement for students to go out on a limb and "dream up" ideas.

Elaboration is the ability to fill out an idea, to add interesting details, and to build up groups of related ideas. To a great extent it is like the synthesis process in the Bloom (1956) *Taxonomy*. Once an idea has been formulated, an individual must be able to bring it to fruition. Elaboration is also important in the fact-finding stage. Once you define an element of the problem, you must be able to clarify and elaborate on how it relates to the conditions of the problem.

This would also be a good time for you to review the material from Chapter 4 on Creative Problem Solving. The six steps of the Creative Problem Solving process (Mess-Finding, Data-Finding, Problem-Finding, Idea-Finding, Solution-Finding, and Acceptance-Finding), and the specific goals and objectives for creative problem solving that were presented in Chapter 4 are important concepts that are basic to keep in mind as you prepare to implement a program. You will probably be able to put these methods to use yourself, as you solve the problems that will arise in planning and starting your own programs.

2. *Be explicit in specifying the processes, skills, and content you want the students in your class to learn and develop.*

In this recommendation we are concerned with developing goal statements and instructional objectives. Some teachers do not believe it is necessary or important to prepare specific instructional objectives. However, planning goals and objectives is an important step in preparing instruction which will effectively foster creative thinking and problem solving.

The development of objectives which contribute to your efforts to foster creative thinking takes into account the content (or subject matter) that will be taught. You should also deliberately consider the processes and abilities in creative thinking and problem solving, and check to insure that you have written objectives which involve the use of those processes and abilities. Some examples of statements of objectives which involve creative-thinking abilities and problem-solving processes have been provided by Covington, Crutchfield, Davis, and Olton (1972) in the Teacher's Guide for the *Productive Thinking Program*. Their summary of the skills of productive thinking includes:

Recognizing puzzling facts
Asking relevant, information-seeking questions
Solving problems in new ways
Generating ideas of high quality
Evaluating ideas
Achieving solutions to problems

The first author of this book has also worked with a school corporation in developing a set of cognitive objectives for a gifted program at the elementary level. They are presented in Figure 5.1. Note that these objectives relate to creativity and problem solving, independence and self direction in learning

1. PRODUCE MULTIPLE IDEAS FOR VARIOUS COGNITIVE TASKS (FLUENCY).

2. THINK OF A WIDE RANGE OF IDEAS FOR DIFFERING TASKS (FLEXIBILITY).

3. BE ORIGINAL AND CREATE RELATIVELY UNIQUE OR INNOVATIVE IDEAS (ORIGINALITY).

4. DEVELOP BASIC IDEAS AND FILL IN INTERESTING AND RELEVANT DETAILS (ELABORATION).

5. ASK QUESTIONS WHICH CLARIFY PUZZLING AND AMBIGUOUS SITUATIONS.

6. USE EFFECTIVE TECHNIQUES IN SOLVING CLOSED (SINGLE SOLUTION) AND OPEN (MULTIPLE SOLUTIONS) PROBLEMS.

7. SYNTHESIZE IDEAS IN CREATIVE PROJECT ACTIVITIES.

8. EVALUATE ALTERNATIVE IDEAS OR SOLUTIONS IN PROBLEM SITUATIONS.

9. SENSE AND CLARIFY PROBLEMS IN A VARIETY OF SITUATIONS.

10. EXERCISE SELF MOTIVATION, DIRECTION, AND INDEPENDENCE IN LEARNING AND PROJECT ACTIVITIES.

11. CARRY OUT AN INDEPENDENT PROGRAM OF FREE READING AT A CHALLENGING LEVEL APPROPRIATE TO THE LEVEL OF READING SKILL.

12. USE LANGUAGE EFFECTIVELY IN SPEAKING AND WRITING.

Figure 5.1. Cognitive objectives for a gifted education program at the elementary level

(10,11) and to language skills (12). In the same project the affective and social goals presented in Figure 5.2 were developed.

In planning what will be taught, we also recommend that you can help encourage creative thinking and problem solving by involving students in making choices and in planning what will be learned. One way to do this is by planning several alternative learning activities, among which the students can choose, for each of your instructional objectives. If you wish to provide the students with an even greater role in planning, you can use class meetings

1. WORK WITH OTHER STUDENTS OF SIMILAR ABILITY IN PROJECT ACTIVITIES.

2. VIEW THEMSELVES AS COMPETENT AND EFFECTIVE LEARNERS.

3. RESPOND POSITIVELY TO VARIOUS TYPES OF COGNITIVE ACTIVITIES (FAVORABLE ATTITUDES TOWARD CREATIVE THINKING, PROBLEM SOLVING AND COGNITIVE PROJECT ACTIVITIES).

4. CLARIFY THEIR OWN VALUES SYSTEMS.

5. VIEW THEMSELVES AS COMPETENT CREATIVE THINKERS, PROBLEM SOLVERS, AND INDEPENDENT LEARNERS.

Figure 5.2. Affective and social goals for a gifted education program at the elementary level

at the beginning of a teaching unit or on a daily basis, at which time the students and the teacher can plan together. This approach can be supplemented very effectively by having another class meeting at the end of the day or unit, in which everyone reviews the progress that has been made and evaluates the extent to which the plans made earlier have been completed. Eventually, of course, the students can be brought into the planning process on an individual basis, through the use of contracts or learning agreements.

As you begin planning a project for developing creative thinking, you should also devote considerable energy to reviewing and selecting useful methods and materials. One source of guidance for task and method selection is Figure 5.3. This chart provides a description of several tasks which promote development in various aspects of problem solving. As you plan your project, a quick glance at the chart will point you in the direction of appropriate activities and tasks. You can use this information by looking to the methods and material available and choosing the materials that utilize the necessary types of activities for your purposes. The task chart is also a helpful tool when you are constructing or devising your own teaching materials.

Using Published Material

One early decision to make involves the extent to which you will utilize published materials, such as those reviewed in Chapter 6. The reviews in Chapter 6 provide enough information to help you make a tentative selection of suitable materials. If you locate some published material that seem to be appropriate for your project, you may be able to arrange to order it through your school's usual channels. (The information provided in the reviews may be helpful to your principal or supply coordinator in ordering the material.)

When the material arrives, scan the whole set to familiarize yourself with it. Then study the teacher's guide or manual quite carefully. The manual usually begins with a description of the purpose or objectives of material, and gives full instructions concerning how to use the kit. You should become thoroughly familiar with the various materials in the kit. Developers of materials often use special terminology when describing their materials. Thus it is imperative that you become familiar with each piece of material being described. This can be accomplished by handling and examining each piece of material as it is being discussed in the teacher's guide.

It is also important to read the complete description of how the material should be used. Some teachers who are highly competent in using traditional instructional material assume that they can bypass much of this material in

Type of Task	Examples of Task Activities
Improvement	1. Product improvement—how could you make this product better. 2. Situation improvement—how could you change this situation, environmental improvement, etc.
"What if" Situations	1. "Just Suppose" imagination activities. Story completion activities. Prediction of consequences.
Observation Activities	1. Finding camouflaged or hidden figures. Scrambled word games, word finding puzzles. 2. Clue finding, information hunting in stories. 3. Problem definition. Defining a problem from a mass of information.
Questioning and Speculation	1. Speculating on what is occurring in a picture or part of a story. 2. Writing newspaper headlines and story titles for pictures. 3. Completing pictures and designs from abstract or symbol line beginnings. 4. Solving riddles and puzzles.
Ideational Fluency	1. Thinking up unusual uses for things, writing as much as possible about absurd topics. 2. Writing similes, synonyms and antonyms for words and phrases. 3. Categorizing—List all of the things you can think of that are cylindrical in shape.

Figure 5.3. Tasks useful in teaching problem awareness and information gathering: Sensitivity and awareness to problems. The discovery of problem situations and problem definition. Organizing available data, asking questions, classifying and utilizing information.

Type of Task	Examples of Task Activities
Flexibility	1. Find a variety of uses for common objects.
	2. Make several drawings from line beginnings. Design symbols for words or ideas.
	3. Indicate subtle changes in phraseology, figural drawings, or visual demonstrations. (Find the figure that is different, where did the change occur, etc.)
	4. Find several solutions to physical puzzles (match stick puzzles, block puzzles, word puzzles.)
	5. Story problems—what endings might this story have, etc.
Elaboration	1. Adding details to drawings, designs, stories, or ideas.
	2. Developing a product such as a model.
Associational Fluency	2. Writing synonyms and antonyms for words.
	2. Producing lists of words that are associated with other words.
Experimentation	1. Manipulation of facts and actual trial of hypotheses through physical experimentation, simulated activities and games, role playing, etc.

Figure 5.3.—*Continued*

the teacher's guide or manual. However, many innovative programs assume completely different teaching strategies emphasizing new methods of presentation, explanation, and student participation. Creativity and problem-solving instructional materials assume that there will be little presentation or explanation by the teacher and much stimulation of independent thinking. Because of the special nature of creativity materials, a thorough understanding of how to use the material to stimulate creative thinking and problem solving is necessary for maximum effectiveness.

The teacher's guide may also describe work that can be done to follow up the work in the kit being used or other sources that will enhance the kit. Clearly, the teacher's guide is a valuable source in which one may find, not only the way in which the kit can be used, but also ways in which auxiliary material or follow up work can be added in the classroom.

The authors of this book, in collaboration with Dr. Joseph Renzulli, have developed a scale for evaluating creativity teaching materials. It contains a concise description of 28 characteristics of creativity teaching materials, in the form of a rating scale that can be useful to you in considering materials for school use. The complete scale, with directions for its use, will be found in Treffinger, Isaksen, & Firestien (1982, pp. 124–126).

Using Methods

You may be interested in utilizing some of the methods for stimulating creative thinking, which were reviewed in Chapter 4. These methods can be useful in your project, whether you decide to make them the principal part of your efforts or whether you incorporate them into a program which also involves the use of published material.

After you have read Chapter 4 and identified some of the methods for possible incorporation in your project, you should plan to devote some additional time to preparation, since you will not have a teacher's manual or ready-made material for the pupils. It is important, of course, that *you* understand the use and limitations of the method. You may find it valuable to consult additional background references from Chapter 4 for any method you plan to try out, since each one involves specific techniques that must be quite clear to you before you will be able to use the method successfully.

When you feel confident that you understand the method, you should give yourself plenty of time to find ways for "building" the method into your instructional plans.

Sometimes the method will be valuable to you in the *planning* stages of instruction. For example, brainstorming can be used with your class to plan the content of a unit or lesson (as was illustrated in Chapter 4). Alternatively, the methods may also be used in developing learning activities for the children, whether individually, in small groups, or with the entire class. Thus, you can use the methods described in Chapter 4 to plan instruction, as well as to provide a basis for learning activities to include in any lesson or unit plan you develop.

3. *Try out your plans and new ideas before you begin to use them with your class.*

It is likely that most teachers will benefit from a trial run through the material as it would be used in the classroom before beginning their actual instruction. While it might seem laborious, this trial use of the material will yield substantial dividends. By doing this you will determine whether you really know how to use the material. Secondly, it allows for teacher anticipation. You have the prized and unmatched vantage point of knowing the needs, desires, problems, abilities, and interests of your students. With that information, plus thorough familiarity with the materials, you can be prepared for questions the students might raise and be able to direct them to follow-up activities. Great benefits can be realized if you direct your students to additional sources or activities when their interest or motivation is high. Furthermore, you can be prepared for the various problems that may arise while conducting the project in the classroom. These problems can range from the need for special equipment to inadequate time allocations for specific activities; they are usually eliminated by careful advance planning.

A trial run can be particularly useful if you are part of a "team-teaching" program, or if you can identify one or more of your colleagues with whom you can share your ideas and plans. If at least two teachers share an interest in a creative-thinking project, there will be many opportunities for the kind of sharing or "cross-fertilization" of ideas that is valuable in creative teaching and learning.

Finally, the trial run may be especially valuable if you are trying out a new method from Chapter 4, since it will provide you with an opportunity to verify your own personal understanding of the method and your ability to use it in your own thinking. You will be much more enthusiastic, probably, if you have had opportunities to put the method to use yourself before you begin to use it with your class.

4. *Create an environment in your class in which creative learning can occur.*

Creative learning does not just happen by chance, and while occasionally it might result from a "happy accident," one should not be satisfied with a project that depends upon luck. In addition, no amount of careful preplanning can reduce the importance of what happens in the classroom when the project actually begins. Every teacher has doubtlessly known the experience of the very carefully planned lesson that falls flat on its face. Fortunately, there are many things you can do to help prevent the fates from determining the success of your project in the classroom. Some of these things are described next under the general category of the "classroom atmosphere" you establish for creative learning.

Warm Up

Before beginning a lesson or activity the teacher should attempt to "warm up" the class. Even the greatest lesson plan will not be effective unless it includes some strategy for establishing a receptive attitude among the students. One effective way of accomplishing this is by using open-ended questions which arouse interest or stimulate curiosity. Another effective approach is to utilize a puzzling phenomenon or problem to stimulate the students to ask their own questions. Many teachers give thought to *asking* different questions, but never think of the possibility of beginning instruction with spontaneous *student* questions. These "warm-up" methods are among those discussed by Torrance and Myers (1970) in their very useful book, *Creative Learning and Teaching.*

Physical Arrangements

One important way of establishing a classroom atmosphere for creative learning is through careful attention to the physical arrangements of the classroom. For example, to use buzz groups effectively, it is necessary to seat small groups of students in circles. In some cases it might be helpful to push the desks aside and have the students sit on the floor. A brainstorming group can be as large as eight to ten students, while other kinds of group discussions, presentations, and demonstration projects may be best suited for an entire class.

If you are using an individualized approach in your project, you will probably also discover that you need to designate various parts of your classroom (or even other nearby rooms if they are available) for a number of individual and group activities throughout the day. If your room is large enough, you may well find it useful to use moveable dividers, portable chalk or bulletin boards, tables, or even home-made wooden or cardboard dividers to partition the room off into various activity areas. It is also worthwhile to include a special area for quiet relaxation and thinking; creative ideas often require a quiet period of time for "incubation."

Physical Activity and Productive Noise

You must also keep in mind that many creative-learning activities involve a greater degree of physical activity and discussion among students than are required by more traditional activities (particularly of the "seat work" variety). In your effort to develop a supportive environment for creative learning, don't work against your own purposes by being too rigid about movement, activity, and noise. There is an important difference, which you can soon learn to distinguish, between disruptive behavior and the "productive noise" and activity of children busily involved in tracking down new ideas and solutions to problems.

A stimulating classroom is filled with resources. There are things to explore, read, study and examine. There are many things on bulletin boards. There are places to relax and talk. The teacher encourages children to talk, to move about, to share ideas. The children do not drift aimlessly. There is no chaos. There is much active pursuit of learning activities. But the atmosphere is relaxed and pleasant. In such a room creativity and problem solving can flourish.

Deferred Judgment

In Chapter 4, in relation to brainstorming, you read about the principle of "deferred judgment." This is also an important principle for the teacher to remember in working to establish a creative learning environment.

Premature and hasty teacher evaluation can destroy a child's first efforts at creativity or problem solving. Creativity and problem solving are risky ventures. There are many blind alleys, false starts, failures, and frustrations. But children must learn to take the risks. This means that teachers must be slow to criticize. They should also help students to learn and practice the deferred judgment principle among themselves and avoid harsh criticism of each other's efforts. Children should also be encouraged to evaluate their own work, and given opportunities to learn how to do it, rather than being totally dependent on the teacher for evaluation.

Learning a Facilitative Role

When teachers first begin to consider the effects of increased student participation in planning, greater student independence in learning activities, and application of the principle of deferred judgment, it is easy for some misunderstandings to occur. Quite frequently, for example, an atmosphere for creative learning is confused with a totally "unstructured" or permissive atmosphere. It is best to avoid the term permissive, for it is extremely value laden and open to too many interpretations. Creative learning does place a great emphasis upon the active role of the learner in managing and directing learning activities independently. In many of the arrangements you develop to foster creativity, children will be somewhat noisier and more active physically than in traditional, self-contained, teacher-centered classrooms. But that does not mean that creative learning leads to children running around, screaming, shouting, or swinging from the light fixtures. Nor does it imply that *learning* is overlooked. In fact, it is true that children involved in creative activities will not only be working toward important goals and objectives, but will also be less likely to resort to aggressive and disruptive behavior.

Of course, the teacher must maintain some control over the class, but a low authority profile will have the most beneficial results. The teacher must act as a guide or facilitator when using creative methods. This means that the methods are student centered and not teacher centered. While relaxing control may be difficult, it is usually an essential ingredient in getting children to think for themselves. At first, the students may not be productive, but with encouragement, patience, and support they will make gains.

If the students believe they can rely on your constant support and encouragement they will be less hesitant to give a response that may not be a popular one. When students are able to give responses that are unpopular and infrequently given by other students, or even funny or ridiculous, they are more likely to think creatively. It is the teacher's responsibility to be accepting of the student's responses, to provide encouragement and reinforcement for all ideas, and to reduce or eliminate the criticism of the other class members. In fact it is better to allow the humor and fun to flow, since this usually accompanies creative ideas. You can help the class most by laughing along with them. This will serve to reinforce the students for their original and flexible thinking and show that you are really serious about encouraging creative thinking.

Teachers must be very open and receptive to the ideas of *all* students. They should not show strong approval of some children's productions while showing disapproval of others that seem silly, funny, or unusual. Both quantity and quality of output will increase when evaluation is eliminated or at least postponed. This contributes to the supportive atmosphere that the teacher should try to foster, and reduces the fear and anxiety that inhibits creative thinking and problem solving in young children. The children must also learn to express appreciation or enjoyment of each others' work while avoiding criticism, ridicule, or sarcasm. The general classroom atmosphere should foster cooperative effort while allowing each child to think independently. The student must feel free to take risks in front of the other students and the teacher, and to express unusual, unique, or different ideas, without fear of ridicule. If students are embarassed or punished for what they say or do, it is not likely that they will make future attempts at thinking and presenting their ideas to classmates.

Finally, when you are attempting to establish a favorable atmosphere for creative thinking and problem solving, you must learn to develop a great deal of patience. You must be able to restrain yourself from "squelching" the child who is a constant source of new ideas. But, by the same token, you must also learn not to inhibit the efforts of students who are slower in getting started. They should also have encouragement, support, and adequate time for thinking about a problem.

In learning a facilitative role, then, it is suggested that you must (1) emphasize the student's self-directed learning as much as possible; (2) maintain a low authority profile; (3) accept ideas, whether common or unusual, from all students; (4) foster in your students and in your own behavior a sense of constructive criticism and an emphasis on self-evaluation processes; (5) strive to eliminate punishment or ridicule of new and unusual ideas; and (6) tolerate differences of time or speed among students in the ability to think up new ideas.

5. *Utilize learning procedures involving many activities and products.*

After your efforts in planning many and varied activities and procedures to help students engage in creative thinking and problem solving, and in developing a facilitative atmosphere, there comes the time when teaching actually starts. Now your challenge is to work with your pupils in ways that will promote the successful attainment of your goals. You will have to work quite regularly at maintaining the classroom environment and helping students employ many different abilities and skills in learning. While this may be a challenge in working with children who have never encountered such efforts before, it is usually very exciting and satisfying for teachers and pupils alike.

There are some things you must be careful to remember, however. First of all, strive to find new and diverse ways for students to express themselves and demonstrate what they are learning. Too often it is easy to restrict ourselves to tests and written reports, although there are many other things pupils can do. You may plan specific alternatives, or allow the students to participate in designing them. Some other products to consider using in your class include: songs and music; murals, sculptures, or paintings; movement and physical expressions; community or school service projects; creation and production of original poetry and drama. Figure 5.4 provides a very extensive list of possible products that can be developed by students. You will find it valuable to en-

A	B	C
Advertisement	Baked goods	Cartoons
Advice column	Ballet	Calendar
Album	Banner	Campaign
Allegory	Batik	Case Study/Case History
Ammonia imprint	Beverage	Catalog
Anagram	Bibliography	Ceramics
Anecdote	Billboard	Charts
Animation	Biography	Checklists
Annotated	Book	Clothing
bibliography	Box	Club
Announcement	Brochure	Code
Anthem	Building	Collage
Apparatus	Bulletin Board	Collection
Aquarium	Business	Comedy
Artifacts		Comic Book
Associations		Community action/service
Audio tapes		Compound
Autobiography		Computer program
Axiom		Conference
		Conference presentation
		Convention
		Costume
		Course of Study
		Crossword

D	E	F
Dance	Editorial	Fabrics
Debate	Energy saving	Fantasy, science fiction
Demonstration	device/plan	Fashions
Design	Equipment	Feature Story
Diagram	Estimate	Film
Diorama	Etching	Filmstrip
Directory	Eulogies	Fiction
Discovery	Experiment	Flags
Display		Flannel boards
Drama		Food
Drawing		Formulas
		Furniture
		Future scenarios

Figure 5.4. Products

G

Gadgets
Gallery
Game
Garment
Gauge
Gift
Glass cutting
Graph
Graphics
Greeting cards

H

Handbills
Handbook
Hatchery
Hats
Headlines
"Helper" services
Hieroglyphics
Histories
Hologram
"Hot Line"

I

Icons
Ideas
Identification charts
(e.g., "Know Your
Fish . . .")
Images
Index
Inscription
Insignia
Instruments
Interviews
Inventions

J

Jamboree
Jazz
Jewelry
Jigsaw puzzle
Jobs
Joke, jokebook
Justification
Journal (personal)
Journal (article)

K

Kaleidoscope
Keepsake
Kit
Knitting

L

Labels
Laboratory
Ladder of ideas
Languages
Latch hooking
Laws
Layouts
Learning centers
Leatherwork
Lei
Lesson
Letter to Editor
Library
List
Lithograph
Log
Looking Glass
Lounge
Lyrics

M

Machine
Macrame
Magazine
Magic Trick
Map
Marquee
Masks
Meetings
Menu
Meter
Mobile
Model
Monument
Mnemonic device
Mural
Museum

N–O

Newsletter
Newspaper
Newspaper ad
News Story
Notice
Novel
Oath
Observance
Observatory
Observation Record
Occupation
Opera
Opinion
Oration
Orchestration
Organization
Origami
Outline

Figure 5.4.—*Continued*

P	Q-R	S
Painting	Quarterly report	Satire
Pamphlet	Query	Scrapbook
Papier maché	Question	Sculpture
Parodies	Questionnaire	Set/scenery
Patterns	Quilling	Short story
Pennants	Quilt	Silk Screen
Petition	Quiz	Simulations
Photograph	Radio Program	Skit
Pillow	Rating	Slide show
Plan	Reaction	Slogan
Poem	Recipe	Song
Poster	Research report	Speech
Prediction	Resolution	Stained Glass
Press release/	Review	Steps
conference	Riddle	Store
Production	Robot	String Art
(show)	Role playing	Stuffed Animal
Prototype		Survey
Puppet		
Puppet show		
Puzzle		

T-U-V	W-X-Y-Z	
Tape recording	Walking tour	Xylographics
Taxonomy	Wall hanging	Yardstick
Television program	Weather map	Yarn (story/fabric)
Term Paper	Weaving	Yearbook
Terrarium	Whittling	Yodel
Test	Wire sculpture	Yo-Yo
Theme	Woodcarving	Zig-Zag
Theory	Woodwork	Zodiac
Tie-dyeing	Word games	Zones
Tool	Written drama	Zoographic studies
Tour	Zerographic	Zoological projects
Toy	print, collage	
Transparencies		
Travelogue		
Uniform		
Unit of study		
Vehicle		
Verse		
Video tape		
Vignette		
Visual Aid		
Volume		
Volunteer program		

Figure 5.4.—*Continued*

courage students to try their hand at expressing themselves in many different ways during a school year.

Although students may be interested in working on projects of their own, and developing a number of new and different kinds of products, they may need assistance from you in learning how to select and develop their ideas and in learning how to conduct specific projects or make certain products. Two useful resources for this purpose are *Choosing and Charting* (Eichberg & Redmond, 1984) and *Pocketful of Projects* (Redmond, 1984).

Creativity and problem solving projects can easily be integrated into the daily classroom routine either as a part of a particular subject area or independently. Many teachers set aside some special time during each day for students to work on their projects as a class, in small groups, or as individuals. If a special time is set aside, you may find it easier to establish a creative atmosphere in the classroom during the period. However, creativity and problem-solving instructional materials can usually fit into any subject area that would normally be taught during the day. Many of the materials and methods described in Chapter 6 are specifically designed to be used as a part of the regular curriculum. Thus the *Purdue Creative Thinking Program* was designed to be used in social studies. Many of the materials are designed for use in language arts and some for use in mathematics and science. When used in this way the materials have dual benefits in that they not only aid in the development of some specific skill or knowledge but they also help to develop creativity or problem solving in students.

The use of small groups gives you and the students many advantages for creative-thinking and problem-solving activities. It reduces the fear and anxiety that may be associated with speaking in front of the whole class. Students are more likely to offer contributions when they are in a small, personal, closely seated group of people. Furthermore, the reduced number of students allows more time for each of the students to be presenting ideas, since each person in the group can talk more often than when the whole class is together. This may be especially helpful for students who speak infrequently or not at all. Small groups also allow students to proceed independently without supervision since the teacher can only visit one group at a time. Small groups can also work at their own pace, going as slow or as fast as is appropriate for the group members.

You should also employ a variety of instructional techniques. Many teachers are already using large and small group discussion, some creative-thinking techniques (such as brainstorming), a wide variety of films and other media, and individualized instructional efforts such as learning centers or learning stations. These can all contribute effectively to creative thinking, problem solving, and inquiry by students. You may find it particularly useful, however, to use a contract or learning agreement approach to help students learn to use instructional resources on their own.

6. *Help students to learn gradually how to use creative thinking and problem solving in dealing with real problems.*

In Chapter Two, we proposed that gifted and talented students should participate in creativity instruction which enables them to plan and conduct independent investigations of real problems and challenges. Many exercises can be offered to students to build their proficiency in divergent thinking, or to give them practice in using "higher level thinking skills" and problem solving processes. These activities and experiences may have some inherent appeal and value in their own right. They may stimulate enjoyment of thinking and learning for example, or they may be experiences that help students practice and learn the vocabulary of effective thinking.

It is our position, however, that we have not fulfilled our instructional responsibilities to gifted and talented students unless we also attempt to assist them in *using* their creative thinking and problem solving skills in dealing effectively with real problems and challenges. Renzulli (1977) emphasized the importance of investigations of real problems as the highest level of "enrichment" for students and Treffinger (1980) described involvement in real problems and challenges as the most complex level of creative learning. Feldhusen and Kolloff (1978) also emphasized the need for teachers to help students deal effectively wtih realistic problems and projects.

In accepting responsibility for helping students learn to be self-directed, to work independently, and to deal with real problems, several new and important challenges will be evident to the teacher or mentor. These include:

1. What is a real problem?
2. How, or from where, do students find and define real problems?
3. What skills are necessary for students to master in order to deal successfully with real problems?
4. What skills are necessary for the teacher or mentor to develop, in order to be an effective facilitator as students learn to deal with real problems?
5. How can we effectively evaluate students' work on real projects?

Each of these questions is very complex, of course, but we will attempt to provide you with some initial guidelines that will be useful as you get started with your students in working on real problems.

What is a real problem? Renzulli (1982) proposed that real problems have a personal frame of reference, that they do not have a known or existing unique solution, that they must be "real" from the personal perspective of the learner (as opposed to someone else), and that they emphasize opportunities for change and contributions. Isaksen and Treffinger (1984) have emphasized three important considerations in "ownership" of a problem: *influence* (is it a problem on which you will really be able to take action?), *interest* (are you really concerned about solving the problem?), and *imagination* (are you willing to approach the problem in a deliberate and systematic problem-solving process?). Real problems come from the person who will be doing the problem solving, not from someone else, and they are problems that the "owner" really cares about!

Where do real problems come from? In one way, we don't find real problems—they find us! Real problems are the challenges and opportunities and difficulties that each of us meets, day in and day out. Sometimes, however, we do want to go looking for opportunities. One way to do that productively is by using what is called in CPS, "an Idea System." An Idea System is any *portable* device that you can use to record ideas, interesting observations, puzzling experiences, or fascinating questions, whenever and wherever they occur to you. A small, pocket-sized spiral notebook, for example, or even a package of 3x5 file cards, can make good Idea Systems. When you review your Idea System on a regular basis, you'll find that it can be an excellent source of interesting and challenging opportunities for real problem solving. At other times, especially in school, we need to look for real problems even more deliberately. Exploring a new area of study, listening to a guest speaker, watching a film, going on a field trip, or just browsing around in a library can be starting points for real problem solving for individual students. Teachers in any school building can promote real problem solving by deliberately working to provide many opportunities for students to pursue interesting and unusual new topics and questions in a variety of different ways and places. Real problems can also be "located" by doing some systematic thinking and planning to explore areas of interest; for these purposes, resources like *Choosing and Charting* (Eichberg and Redmond, 1984) can be very useful.

What skills are needed by students? In order to become effective in dealing with real problems, your students will need to learn how to find and define problems, locate and use references and information sources, work effectively with a variety of other people, obtain the support and resources needed to carry out a project, develop craftsmanship and high standards, create products, locate audiences and opportunities for sharing their work, derive personal and intellectual satisfaction from their own work, and overcome obstacles and frustration (Treffinger, Isaksen, & Firestien, 1982, pp. 67–69; Gross, 1982). They will also need to have had exposure to a variety of "tools" for effective thinking and practice in using those tools effectively; it doesn't work very well to go fishing without bait or hooks! These are complex skills, and you should not expect that every student will develop them quickly or easily; indeed, some students may only be prepared and motivated for real problem solving after much patient guidance and waiting! It is important to remember that you should not expect *every* student to "crank out" wonderful and unique projects on a fixed schedule, like some kind of "independent study assembly line." The real world of problem solving just doesn't work that way. It is also important for you to spend some time with your students to help them define the steps that must be undertaken in a real project, and to help them learn how to monitor their own accomplishment of those steps.

What skills does the teacher need? For each step that students must take in the process of learning to solve real problems, there is a corresponding set of challenges for the teacher. First, you must recognize that you will need to function as a *facilitator* of the student's efforts, not as a dispenser of knowledge. You will also have to remind yourself at first that it isn't your job to solve the problem for the student. Thus, you will find that it will be necessary for you to function in some ways that are very different from what you do in "teaching content" to the students. Renzulli (1983) has emphasized the important role of the teacher in relation to problem-finding and focussing; serving as a "managerial assistant;" providing feedback and encouragement; and helping students locate appropriate outlets for their work. Isaksen (1983) has also defined specific goals and objectives for facilitators of creative problem solving, emphasizing five important dimensions: establishing and maintaining a supportive environment; defining, differentiating, and internalizing the facilitator's role and responsibilities; defining and differentiating the client's [i.e., students'] roles and responsibilities; specifying task dimensions; and understanding the dynamics of all elements of facilitation. Effective management and direction of real problem solving by students also involves creativity and imagination in organizing and using classroom space, furniture, and instructional resources in a facilitative way (e.g., Dunn & Dunn, 1978; Feldhusen, 1981).

How can students' work be evaluated? Evaluation of students' real problem solving efforts presents a problem for some teachers, because it does not readily lend itself to the usual methods we employ for evaluating students. If the student's investigation begins with intensive and detailed Fact-Finding in a specific content area that is related to one or more components of the basic curriculum, then it is possible that you might discover gains in test scores (such as teacher-made unit tests or standardized achievement tests). It is much more likely, however, that the students' investigation of real problems will draw them deeply into more advanced and specialized areas of investigation, and into very specific problem statements that do not "match" the lower-level objectives assessed by most objective tests. That is not to say that the students are not learning much new and worthwhile information (even at basic knowledge and comprehension levels) in the course of their investigation; rather, it is merely to point out that such knowledge may or may not "match" very well with the specific content objectives established for a particular basic unit of instruction, teacher made test, or standardized test. It is important, nonetheless, for us to be able to verify and document the students' actual learning and accomplishments. The first way to do this is through careful documentation of the products and solutions and the audiences or outlets with whom they

Name _____ Project Title _____

1. WHAT DO YOU LIKE BEST ABOUT YOUR PROJECT? WHY? _____

   _____

2. WHAT WERE THE MOST DIFFICULT STEPS? HOW DID YOU
   OVERCOME THE DIFFICULTIES? _____

   _____

   _____

3. NAME SOME NEW SKILLS YOU LEARNED IN WORKING ON THIS
   PROJECT:

   _____

   _____

4. IN WHAT WAYS WAS YOUR PLAN OF ACTION REASONABLE? IN
   WHAT WAYS MIGHT YOU HAVE IMPROVED YOUR PLAN?
   WAYS IT WAS REASONABLE: __   POSSIBLE IMPROVEMENTS: __

   _____   _____

   _____   _____

   _____   _____

   _____   _____

5. WHO ELSE WAS INTERESTED IN YOUR PROJECT? WITH WHOM
   DID YOU SHARE YOUR RESULTS, AND HOW?

   _____

   _____

   _____

6. WHAT NEW IDEAS FOR PROJECTS OR UNANSWERED QUESTIONS
   ABOUT THE TOPIC DO YOU STILL HAVE?

   _____

   _____

   _____

7. ALL THINGS CONSIDERED, HOW SUCCESSFUL WAS YOUR
   STUDY? (ADD ANY ADDITIONAL COMMENTS OR QUESTIONS ON
   THE BACK OF THIS PAGE)

   _____

   _____

   _____

Figure 5.5. Independent study evaluation form

have been shared. Real problems lead to real solutions; the very implementation of those solutions, documented, for example, through a scrapbook or photo essay or with letters from supervisors, sponsors or audience members, can provide impressive "evidence" of the student's success. If you also want to have some simple, written evaluation of the students' work, you might investigate the use of Independent Study Folders (Homeratha & Treffinger, 1980), in which specific records of activities, learning experiences, and evaluation criteria are maintained. Figures 5.5 and 5.6 provide samples of two basic evaluation forms.

7. *Conduct a careful review and evaluation, not only of the students' learning, but of your own project and efforts, and plan revisions accordingly.*

Your first concern in evaluation will probably be to seek effective ways of assessing the students' performance, and it is certainly necessary to do this. Creative learning does not imply that any concern for evaluation is dismissed. Although it is important to learn to *defer* judgment, there must come a time when you get down to the process of making decisions and assessing the quality of ideas and solutions. In relation to evaluation of the students, there are three specific suggestions you should consider. First, learn to define and use new sources of "evidence" in your evaluation. Do not feel constrained to evaluation using paper and pencil test scores and reports. By adopting a broad definition of evaluation, the questions you are striving to answer are: "Has the student reached the goal? How well has the job been done? What kinds of data do I have to support the decision?" Be alert, therefore, for *any* kinds of data to document the attainment of the goals and objectives by the students. Figure 5.5 presents a form which can by used by students for self evaluation of any independent study project; and Figure 5.6 is a form to be used by the students in evaluating a presentation of an independent study project.

Second, learn to use criterion-referenced evaluation, not just norm-referenced. It is not always necessary to compare students with each other. In creative-learning outcomes, it may frequently be much more appropriate to assess the *change* or *progress* made by the learner from one time to another, or to examine the success of the learner's efforts in relation to the specific goals that were defined. Third, the evaluation of creative learning and problem solving should increasingly be conducted *by the learner*.

You should also be concerned with evaluating your entire project. You may find it valuable to do this on a day-to-day basis and not just at the completion of the entire project. Again, you should begin by going back to the general goals of the project: why did you begin the project initially? What were you hoping to accomplish? Then, for each of your responses to these questions, ask yourself, "what kind of evidence would indicate whether or not that has actually happened?"

An important aspect of evaluation, which you should also remember, is that one purpose of evaluation is to provide you with a basis for systematic

| Presentor's Names _____ Date _____ |
| Evaluator's Name _____ |
| Project Title _____ |

FOR EACH OF THESE CRITERIA, RATE THE PRESENTATION USING THE FOLLOWING SCALE: 4-EXCELLENT 3-GOOD 2-FAIR 1-POOR

I. CONTENT		II. PRESENTATION	
PROBLEM WELL-STATED?	_____	METHOD OF PRESENTING APPROPRIATE?	_____
CLEAR GOALS/ OBJECTIVES?	_____	EFFECTIVE ORGANIZATION AND SEQUENCE?	_____
INFORMATION SOURCES IDENTIFIED SPECIFICALLY?	_____	EVIDENCE OF GOOD USE OF ORAL/WRITTEN LANGUAGE SKILLS?	_____
VARIETY OF SOURCES?	_____	USE OF VISUAL AIDS AND/OR HANDOUTS?	_____
APPROPRIATE METHODS OF INVESTIGATION?	_____	ALL MATERIALS AND EQUIPMENT AVAILABLE?	_____
GOOD ORGANIZATION?	_____	PRESENTER INTERESTED, ALERT, POISED?	_____
ORIGINAL IDEAS?	_____		
OTHER: _____	_____	AUDIENCE INVOLVED?	_____
_____	_____	OTHER: _____	_____
_____	_____	_____	_____
SUB-TOTAL:	_____	SUB-TOTAL:	_____

Figure 5.6. Evaluation Form

revisions of the program. Thus, after you have collected the evidence to evaluate your project, don't just use it to say, "It worked," or "It didn't work very well," and then drop it at that. Instead, seek to probe the strengths and weaknesses of the program, and try to look specifically at each factor thus identified. How can you improve the strengths? What can be done to revise the weaknesses? What new ideas should be incorporated?

Some Things to Watch Out for

No matter how careful your planning and attention to the basic guidelines, things can go wrong. You cannot be protected from those problems and aggravations that can accompany any approach to instruction. But there are some things that you should be warned about, in the hope that forewarned will be forearmed.

III. OUTCOMES

WERE OBJECTIVES OF THE
STUDY ATTAINED? _____

BENEFIT OF THE STUDY
TO PRESENTER _____

BENEFIT TO ANYONE
ELSE (AUDIENCE) _____

LEAD TO NEW IDEAS
FOR FUTURE STUDY? _____

OTHER: _____ _____

_____ _____

SUB-TOTAL: _____

IV. YOUR SUMMARY

WHAT WERE THE STRONGEST/
WEAKEST ASPECTS OF THIS
PRESENTATION?

STRONGEST:

_____

_____

_____

WEAKEST:

_____

_____

_____

Use back for additional comments

TOTAL EVALUATION PART I _____ OUT OF POSSIBLE _____

II

III _____ OUT OF POSSIBLE _____

TOTAL:

_____ OUT OF POSSIBLE _____

_____ OUT OF POSSIBLE _____

Figure 5.6.—*Continued*

First of all, don't give up when your first efforts are rough around the edges. Give yourself a fair chance to grow and to develop your own creative abilities. Too many times educational projects are dropped prematurely, with the first signs of difficulty, only later to have someone say, "Oh yes, I did try that once, and it wasn't any good." You must not be overcome with the frustration of a first attempt, but remember that with more experience, success will be easier to attain.

Second, creative thinking and problem solving, like any other educational concerns, can be handled in such a way as to become dull, boring routines. Your students will need variety, and there will be pressure upon you to create new ideas, and to keep on creating. Creative learning is not a venture for the teacher who wants to build a neat little package to use the same way, day in and day out. You will have to be prepared to work very hard to be flexible and original yourself.

Third, you will have to be flexible in responding to many more spontaneous, original ideas from your pupils. You won't have the cushion of the right answers in the teacher's guide to fall back upon. There will be times when you will have to say, "I don't know," and these occasions can be threatening to some people.

Fourth, you will have to deal with many more variations in time and daily schedules. Creative thinking and problem solving do take time. Individualized learning means that many children will be pursuing many different projects and activities throughout the day. At first, this may seem to be a state of chaos or disarray, but as you become more confident of the learner's efforts and your own organization, it will become much easier for you to tolerate.

Fifth, you must be prepared to create and maintain a constantly changing and growing pool of resources for learning. It won't do to put the goblins and witches up on the bulletin board in October and leave them there until the turkeys go up at the end of November. Nor will the reading table be adequately stocked with a few old books to last the year. There must be many different resources, and you will have to work hard to see that they are up-to-date and well suited to the changing interests and activities of the students.

Sixth, you may find that some of the traditional behaviors of teaching are difficult to change, particularly those which involve evaluation. When you look at someone's work, there may often be that persistent tendency to say, "Well, here's what you should do to correct this and that . . ." or "Let's see—this word is spelled wrong, and that idea isn't clear. . . ." It is difficult to learn to defer judgment, even when you know that eventually, evaluation will still occur. This will be a challenge to your own creative ability.

Seventh, it may be difficult at first to keep in mind that every child has the potential for creative thinking and problem solving. One must be concerned not only with a few children who display exceptional creative talent, but with providing opportunities for every child to develop these abilities and skills.

Eighth, some creative-thinking activities may be viewed by children as sex-typed. Creative dance, art, and poetry are viewed by some boys as girlish activities while mechanics, science, and sports are viewed by some girls as boy-type activities. Special efforts are needed by the teacher to overcome these sex-oriented responses. Above all, all creative and problem-solving activities should be experienced by both boys and girls. If the experience is rewarding, most of the problems will be overcome or at least alleviated.

Ninth, creativity and problem-solving methods and materials will demand a higher level of creative preparation from the teacher than traditional methods and materials. You will not be able simply to "follow the manual." More creative effort is needed to plan lessons, find materials, and guide ongoing learning activities.

Finally, you must make some decisions about your own values and commitments. You will be able to be most successful if you are concerned with fostering intellectual and personal growth in the individual child. You cannot view your job as mechanically "facing the little monsters every day" to get a paycheck if you are going to be successful in fostering creative learning, inquiry, and problem solving.

Summary

The ideas presented in this chapter imply careful, systematic planning of instruction. Some teachers will want more specific guidance. Thus, we refer you to another publication titled *Reach Each You Teach* by Treffinger, Hohn and Feldhusen (1979). This book offers a comprehensive set of procedures, with illustrations, for developing instructional plans. It also focuses on how to plan for individualized instruction and on striving for higher level thinking processes in teaching.

Chapter 6

REVIEWS OF INSTRUCTIONAL MATERIAL AND BOOKS FOR TEACHING CREATIVITY AND PROBLEM SOLVING

This chapter presents the reviews of instructional materials and books on teaching creative thinking. The reviews of instructional material contain much specific information. Look at a sample review in that section. Then look at the headings described in Figure I. To the right of the headings are explanations of what each word or words mean.

The reviews will give you all the information you need to make a tentative decision as to the suitability of a kit or set of materials for your needs and interests. All of the reviews describe good, useful, productive instructional materials. Materials were included only after a careful inspection and review of a set indicated that it would be useful in teaching creative thinking or problem solving. When you settle on some materials which look interesting, you should read the entire review carefully.

The reviews of books on teaching creative thinking and problem solving are grouped together at the end of the chapter. These reviews attempt to show how each book would be useful to the classroom teacher.

Figure I
The Format of a Review of
Instructional Material

What:	This gives the title of the material and the author.
Published By:	This is the name of the company publishing the material and their mailing address.
How To Order:	This part gives three pieces of information. The first will tell you where to send your orders. Usually this will be the publisher unless otherwise indicated. If it is the publisher it will say "Order from publisher." Use the address given above in the "Published By" section. The second bit of information is the price of the material at the time it was reviewed. The final bit of information tells what item or parts of the material will be expended or lost as the kit is used in the classroom.
Description:	This section gives a brief description of the material, how it is used, and its most salient characteristics.
Target Audience:	This section describes the grade level for which the material is intended.
Materials Provided:	This section tells the quantity of the materials provided and names each piece that will come with the kit.
Teacher's Guide:	If the kit contains a teacher's guide, this section will describe the guide and tell what you can expect from it.
Subject Matter and Teaching Strategy:	This section describes how the material can be used in a variety of subject areas. You can use this information to plan how you will integrate a kit into your daily schedule, or use it to plan for creativity sessions in your classroom. The teaching strategy describes the suggested sequence of events that the teacher could use to teach a class.
Rationale:	Here the fundamental nature of the material is discussed. Its theoretical bases are described.

What:	*Affective Direction—Planning and Teaching for Thinking and Feeling* Bob Eberle and Rosie Hall
Published By:	DOK Publishers, Inc. P.O. Box 605 East Aurora, N.Y. 14052
How To Order:	Order from publisher List price: $9.95 Consumable items: None
Description:	*Affective Direction* is a working book for teachers, taking them progressively through the cognitive and affective processes in concise outline form. The book directs the reader through curriculum planning and classroom instruction, keeping in mind the authors aims—aesthetic sensitivity, interpersonal relations, moral-ethical development, and self-knowledge.
Target Audience:	Elementary and junior high school
Materials Provided:	One *Affective Direction* book
Teacher's Guide:	The entire book is intended to be used as a teacher's guide to the affective domain.
Subject Matter and Teaching Strategy:	The overall purpose of the book is to help educators teach for ethical and moral behavior. Several relevant goals are subsumed under the general purpose, including the aiding or understanding of the affective domain, the development of a general planning and teaching model, the classification and organization of instructional material from a design based on developmental theory, and the provision to teachers of a sense of direction in preparing instructional units. "Guideposts" and "checkpoints" provide the reader with a sense of direction and organization as he or she works through the book. A planning and teaching model is provided based on the cognitive and affective taxonomies. The model is based on the dimensions of content, processes, and strategies.

Affective Direction may be used in several ways by the individual teacher interested in providing for student cognitive, affective, and personal growth, by teams of teachers organizing instruction, by curriculum planners, by teachers of the gifted focusing on higher level thinking and feeling processes, and by teachers interested in developing creativity in students.

Rationale: The authors believe that an individual's self-concept, interpersonal relations, and aesthetic sensitivity largely determine motivation and achievement levels. Development of the capacity to intellectualize has long been the domain of education. Educators are now being held accountable for solving many of society's ills, and affective goals have recently become a major responsibility of teachers. This book aids the teacher in understanding the need for affective education and in learning how to provide for it.

What:	*Affective Education Guidebook* Bob Eberle and Rosie Hall
Published-By:	DOK Publishers, Inc. P.O. Box 605 East Aurora, N.Y. 14052
How To *Order:*	Order from publisher. List price: $9.95
Description:	The *Affective Education Guidebook* is a well-organized set of activities and instructional plans for teachers who are concerned with improving students' understanding and expression of feelings in the classroom setting. It contains more than 100 useful activities as well as suggestions for their effective utilization in the classroom.
Target *Audience:*	Elementary and Junior High School.
Materials *Provided:*	The *Affective Education Guidebook* presents a rationale for concern with affective education, an outline for a general plan (emphasizing program orientation, program planning, and program implementation), and more than 100 specific classroom activities. In addition, there are Appendices which emphasize group discussion skills, problem-solving guidelines, a plan for "building classroom community," and classroom techniques for relaxing and reflecting.
Teacher's *Guide:*	The *Affective Education Guidebook* is directed to the teacher, but it contains specific ideas and plans for classroom application too.
Subject *Matter* *and* *Teaching* *Strategy:*	The *Guidebook's* resources are intended to deal generally with the need to improve human relationships in the classroom. It should be considered resource material for "Affective Education." There are five levels represented in these resources: identification of many different feelings; steps toward the expression of feelings; provision for interaction and discussion of interpersonal relationships; new ways of exploring feelings; and authentic expressions of interpersonal regard.

Rationale: Drawing from the cognitive and affective taxonomies, and from the work of Frank Williams and others, the authors emphasize the ultimate goal of "a *community,* in which interpersonal bonds have been established, a higher level of human nature exists, and the sharing of psychic energy becomes possible" (p. 11).

What:	*Apple Shines: Polishing Student Writing Skills,* by Bob Eberle
Published By:	Good Apple, Inc. P.O. Box 299 Carthage, IL 62321–0299
How To Order:	Order from publisher $7.95 Contains reproducible pages.
Description:	*Apple Shines* contains "think-and-then-write" activities for every week of the school year. Through creative involvement, students are encouraged to express original ideas and use them in writing.
Target Audience:	Grades 4–8
Materials Provided:	The booklet contains more than 40 exercises for students, four brief notes to young writers by professional writers, and many reproducible pages and resources.
Teacher's Guide:	An introduction, instructions, and suggestions for follow-up are provided for each exercise.
Subject Matter And Teaching Strategy:	The activities in this book use many strategies to promote higher level thinking processes and creative expression, and can be used as individual, small group, or whole class activities. Students are provided a number of alternative writing activities from which to choose.
Rationale:	The book attempts to help young writers "polish" their skills and develop creative products in an interesting and enjoyable format.

What:	*Astrogation License*
	Edith J. S. Doherty and Louise C. Evans

Published By: Synergetics
P.O. Box 84
East Windsor Hill, CT 06028

How To Order: Order from publisher
List Price: $15.00

Description: *Astrogation License* is a math and science unit based upon NASA data. While advancing through self-programmed instruction from space cadet to chief astrogator, students learn to navigate in space. Teachers are provided with 5 learning centers with 16 multi-disciplinary activities; background information on planetary time and rocketry; explanations for solutions and all mathematical answers; and suggested alternative sequences for grades 3–4, 5–6, and 7–10.

Target Audience: Grades 3 through 10

Materials Provided: This 8½″ × 11″ book of 149 pages includes all the information and lessons needed to teach this curriculum unit.

Teacher's Guide: This guide is a detailed study of rocketry and navigation in space. The teacher is given an organized sequence of activities that introduce the planets, stars, comets, galaxies, and other astronomical bodies, plus the concepts of gravity, planetary time, Newton's Laws of Motion, a light year, retrograde motion, parallax, and mathematical relationships such as mass ratio, specific impulse, exhaust velocity, and launch vehicle velocity. Students with the knowledge of only the basic four arithmetic operations can solve a majority of the mathematical problems in physics and astronomy and learn how to navigate in space. For the mathematically and scientifically gifted, added levels of difficulty which require a knowledge of decimals, logarithms, and trigonometry are supplied. Background knowledge with easy-to-understand examples are provided to teach these concepts to students.

Subject Matter *and Teaching* *Strategy:* This unit is a part of the Independent Study Process (I.S.P.). The I.S.P. has three phases: Teacher-Led, Independent Study, and Seminar. In the teacher-led phase, the teacher introduces the depth and breadth of an academic area. Then the student picks a topic that interests him/her and completes an independent study. The seminar teaches complicated skills such as computer programming, photography, and the Creative Problem-Solving Process. This guide is one of the learning centers to a futuristics, astronomy, or physics teacher-led unit. It can be used with gifted in a regular classroom, in a resource room, or as a project for two or three students.

Rationale: This guide is based upon the curriculum principles of Taba. Students are taught an organized structure of knowledge and skills to promote retention and transfer. The theories of Renzulli and the creative and cognitive skills of Williams, Bloom, Taylor, and Parnes are incorporated in this cohesive curriculum unit.

What:	*Basic Thinking Skills* Anita Harnadek
Published by:	Midwest Publications PO Box 448 Dept. 70 Pacific Grove, CA 93950
How to Order:	Order from Publishers List Price: $4.75 each book $9.95 includes dittos
Description:	Activities designed to sharpen analytical thinking skills are provided. The twelve books are supplementary, non-graded, low-read, and interdisciplinary. The thinking skills involved can be related to Bloom's Taxonomy, Guilford's Structure of the Intellect, and are valid for Mary Meeker's SOI.
Target Audience:	Gifted first grade to adult.
Materials Provided:	Each volume focuses on one particular skill, and activities are designed to focus on a specific level of difficulty. The following may be purchased individually: Analogies A Analogies B Analogies C Antonyms and Synonyms Antonyms and Synonyms, Similarities and Differences Following Directions = A Following Directions = B Miscellaneous Including Transitivity and Same Person or Not? Patterns Think About It What Would You Do? And True to Life or Fantasy
Subject Matter And Teaching Strategy	For the best transfer of thinking skills to the various disciplines, it is suggested that the exercises be done with the entire class and be solved through class discussion. This method enables the teacher to work on listening skills and permits weak readers to participate in the thinking process.

Rationale: The purpose of the *Basic Thinking Skills* series is to sharpen analytical thinking for better reading comprehension, math, writing, science, test taking, etc.

What:	*Choosing and Charting* Janice K. Eichbers and Lindy T. Redmond *Pocketful of Projects* Lindy T. Redmond
Published By:	Center for Creative Learning PO Box 619 Honeoye, New York 14471
How To: Order:	Order from publisher by title. List price: $12.00 each, $20.00 for both.
Description:	*Choosing and Charting* assists students in selecting study topics of personal interest. It includes a variety of self-awareness questionnaires and provides teachers with guidelines to assist students in selecting projects. *Pocketful of Projects* describes general methods for obtaining information from the community as well as libraries. It also lists many project ideas and directions for students to follow in their discovery of knowledge. Finally, instructions for doing various projects are included. Both books include copies of student worksheets which may be duplicated by teachers for use in the classroom.
Target Audience:	Teachers, grades 3–12. Individual use has also been made of the materials with younger children who are very able.
Materials Provided:	A three ring notebook with instructions for teachers. Student activity sheets are also included which may be duplicated for classroom use.
Subject Matter and Teaching Strategy:	Activities are designed to guide students through the selection of an appropriate topic, discovery of information, and completion of an imaginative product. Several ideas are presented which have been successfully used by students.
Rationale:	Gifted students should be encouraged to develop independent study habits. Students require some structure, however, in the selection of and the development of an imaginative product. This book contains ideas which assist students in going beyond merely reporting information.

What:	*CPS for Kids* by Bob Eberle and Bob Stanish
Published By:	DOK Publishing Co. P.O. Box 605 East Aurora, NY 14052
How To Order:	Order from publisher List Price: $8.95 Includes many reproducible pages
Description:	*CPS for Kids* is an excellent resource for introducing students to the creative problem solving process. It provides specific exercises and activities for each CPS stage.
Target Audience:	Intermediate and middle grades (4–8)
Materials Provided:	The booklet contains exercises, each on a reproducible page, spanning each stage of CPS from objective or mess finding through acceptance finding.
Teacher's Guide:	There are specific instructions for using each activity provided for the teacher. It is desirable, however, for the teacher to know the CPS model before using these materials.
Subject Matter And Teaching Strategy:	This book helps to teach students the specific thinking skills or "process tools" they will need to be able to use creative problem solving methods for real problems. Rather than relating to any specific subject or content areas, the exercises and activities use a wide variety of practical, everyday situations and many fanciful, imaginatve concepts to guide the students in developing process skills.
Rationale:	This book represents one of the most effective resources available for using the Creative Problem Solving Model (described in Chapter 4) with elementary and middle school students. It builds upon the rationale that students can learn to solve problems more creatively by learning and applying deliberate strategies or methods.

What:	*Creativity in Life Science* Patricia Fulmer
Published By:	DOK Publishing Co. P.O. Box 605 East Aurora, NY 14052
How To Order:	Order from publisher List Price: $3.95
Description:	Thirty-six activities to stimulate creative thinking in a variety of specific topics in life sciences.
Target Audience:	Grades 3–8
Materials Provided:	Thirty-six activity cards, each addressed to a specific topic in life science areas, and each designed to employ specific teaching strategies to promote cognitive or affective dimensions of creativity.
Teacher's Guide:	None
Subject Matter/ Teaching Strategy:	A variety of specific strategies are suggested. The subject matter is the life sciences.
Rationale:	Based on Williams' model for encouraging thinking and feeling.

What:	*Creative Problem Solving for an Eency Weency Spider* Gretchen A. Duling
Published By:	DOK Publishing Co. P.O. Box 605 East Aurora, NY 14052
How *To* *Order:*	Order from the publisher $3.95 for Teacher's book including student activity book; additional student books are $6.25/pkg. of 5; class set $26.25.
Description:	A brief explanation of the Osborn-Parnes CPS process in simple language, with several activities for primary age children.
Target *Audience:*	Grades K–3
Materials *Provided:*	Twelve page booklet plus twelve page student activity booklet.
Teacher's *Guide:*	Booklet reviews CPS steps and provides suggestions for effective classroom use with young children.
Subject Matter/ *Teaching* *Strategy:*	A variety of teaching activities are employed that can be used successfully with younger children, including stories, drawings, and songs.
Rationale:	Based on the Osborn-Parnes CPS model.

What:	*Critical Thinking: Book One*
	Critical Thinking: Book Two
	Anita Harnadek
Published by:	Midwest Publications
	PO Box 448 Dept. 70
	Pacific Grove, CA 93950
How to Order:	Order from publisher
	List price: $9.95 Book I
	$4.95 Book I Teacher's Manual
	$10.95 Book II
	$5.95 Book II Teacher's Manual

Description: *Critical Thinking-Book I* involves students in the reasoning process and is not limited to particular subject areas. Activities can be related to Bloom's Taxonomy. Guilford's Structure of the Intellect and is validated for Mary Meeker's S.O.I.

    Critical Thinking-Book II discourages nit-picking and insists instead that the students try to decide what is probably meant, true, assumed to be true, or intended. Drawing on newspaper articles, letters to editors, advice columns and commentaries, and on newscasts, ads, ordinary conversations, political speeches and government regulations as well as other sources, students are presented with a variety of ordinary life situations to consider.

Target Audience: Gifted upper elementary to lower college

Material Provided: There are 200 examples and 1000 problems and questions from which to choose in *Critical Thinking-Book II*.

    Containing over 360 examples and 2100 problems and questions, *Critical Thinking, Book 2* takes up where the first book leaves off.

Subject Matter and Teaching Strategy: The primary teaching approach in this series, is class discussion. The material may be used for supplementary activities in almost any course. However, these books make very good "mini" or semester courses taught by one or several disciplines or departments. Class discussion and argument are used for the best transfer of thinking skill to the various disciplines or skills. These books are also nongraded.

Rationale: The purpose of *Critical Thinking Book I* is to sharpen thinking skills, using class discussion. The author tried to take advantage of the fact that most gifted students love class discussion and arguments.

The objective of *Creative Thinking-Book II* is to sharpen thinking skills for better reading comprehension, math, writing, science, communication, test taking, etc. In this book the questions asked are more probing, and the analyses required are more subtle than asked for in the first volume.

What:	*Fact, Fantasy and Folklore* Greta B. Lipson and Baxter Morrison
Published By:	Good Apple, Inc. Box 299 Carthage, Illinois 62321
How To Order:	Order from publisher List price: $9.95 Consumable items: None
Description:	This ingenious book consists of eleven folk tales and related activities for use in language arts classes. One significant issue has been identified for each story, and students are shown a different perspective on the story and the issue, thus requiring them to see alternative sides to a problem. The book is designed to develop skills in reading, writing, listening, oral expression, and valuing and to foster critical thinking.
Target Audience:	Grades 3–12
Materials Provided:	One *Fact, Fantasy and Folklore* book
Subject Matter and Teaching Strategy:	Although *Fact, Fantasy and Folklore* is specifically designed for use in language arts, the teacher may take an interdisciplinary approach by considering other areas, such as social studies, as well. Students read and discuss the tales, and are encouraged to challenge the conventional acceptance of an issue. Besides stimulating critical discussion, each unit contains such activities as role playing and improvisational drama. The teacher is provided with background clues to aid in developing major lesson plans.
Rationale:	Looking at stories from a new perspective invites divergent thinking and imagination building. Understanding a different approach to everyday values is fun for students and, at the same time, aids greatly in developing creative thought, especially flexibility.

What:	*Flights of Fantasy* Lorraine Plum
Published By:	Good Apple, Inc. P.O. Box 299 Carthage, IL 62321
How To Order:	Order from publisher List Price: $5.95 Record, cassette available, $8.95 each
Description:	*Flights of Fantasy* contains 50 reproducible pages designed to enhance and refine student's natural inclination to image and fantasize.
Target Audience:	All grade levels.
Materials Provided:	One *Flights of Fantasy* book with reproducible activities.
Subject Matter And Treaching Strategy:	The book deals with these strategies: visualization, relaxation and concentration, self-image, and guided fantasy. These techniques may be used with any children of any age level. The strategies are incorporated into activities which are designed to take on these forms: discussion, creative writing, art work, music, research, and others.
Rationale:	*Flights of Fantasy* has grown out of a deep conviction that "learning becomes meaningful and integrated only when we provide a balance in the types of educational experiences we offer students. Only when we consciously and consistently provide experiences that acknowledge the body, the feelings, and the spirit, and honor both hemispheric functions of the brain, can we say with any sense of integrity that we are striving to develop 'the whole person'."

What:	*The Good Apple Creative Writing Book* Gary Grimm and Don Mitchell
Published By:	Good Apple, Inc. Box 299 Carthage, Illinois 62321
How To Order:	Order from publisher List price: $7.95 Consumable items: None
Description:	*The Good Apple Creative Writing Book* provides children with the opportunity to increase their creative thinking and writing skills through the use of divergent and evaluative activities in a format which is practical, easy-to-use and reasonably priced.
Target Audience:	Grades 3–6
Materials Provided:	One *Creative Writing Book*
Subject Matter and Teaching Strategy:	The activities are designed to provide teachers and students with alternative approaches to creative writing, emphasizing that flexibility is a necessary component in developing creative writing abilities. Several relevant topics are suggested, such as magazine interviews, advertisement, autobiographies, a symbol dictionary and travel brochures, to teach practical concepts of current interest to students in a creative and imaginative fashion.
Rationale:	Most classroom materials give first priority to the development of convergent thinking skills. The authors of *The Good Apple Creative Writing Book* believe that divergent and evaluative thinking abilities are equally important to the educational process, but are often ignored. These skills may be more important than the more logical, fact-finding process of convergent thinking to help students meet their continually changing environments.

What:	*Good Apple Records*
Published By:	Good Apple, Inc. Box 299 Carthage, Illinois 62321
How To Order:	Order from publisher List Price: $8.95 each record, $5.95 each book. Consumable items: None Cassettes are available $8.95
Description:	Good Apple Records combine appealing children's songs with divergent activities to stimulate the creative thinking skills of fluency, flexibility, originality, and elaboration.
Target Audience:	Grades Kindergarten–6
Materials Provided:	One Good Apple record plus one activity book per set. Record ($6.95) and book ($5.95) sets include: *Dandy-Lions Never Roar,* by Joe Wayman and Don Mitchell: This album stresses divergent thinking and self-concept building through such songs as "Spiders, Bugs 'n Snakes" and "I Have Feelings." Large group brainstorming activities and individual exercises that relate to each song are provided. *Imagination and Me,* by Joe Wayman and Don Mitchell: This album explores the potential for imagination that rests in every child. Self concept is also stressed through, "I Like Me" and "If You Think You Can or If You Think You Can't, Your're Absolutely Right."
Teacher's Guide:	The activity book provided with each record explains creativity and discusses examples of fluency, flexibility, and originality, and elaboration. Several pages offer suggested activities to use with the records for further creativity stimulation.
Subject Matter and Teaching Strategy:	Development of creative thinking in students as well as self-concept building are the aims of the records. Teaching strategies are flexible. The authors suggest possible plans for class use. The first days of a new song involve listening to, singing and dancing with and discussing the song. Teachers may then duplicate pages from

121

the activity book corresponding with the song, and the following days may involve working on activities and sharing results.

Rationale: Music is a natural motivator to all children. By using music as an aid to imagination development, children become more creative and spontaneous in their thoughts and actions.

What:	*Grokking into the Future* Edith J. S. Doherty and Louise C. Evans
Published *By:*	Synergetics P.O. Box 84 East Windsor Hill, Ct 06028
How *To* *Order:*	Order from publisher List Price: $24.95 (Teacher's Guide) $5.00 (Student/Teacher Packet #2 or Task Cards Packet #1, $7.95 Individual Student Learning Centers Packet #4, if purchased alone)
Description:	*Grokking into the Future* is a simulation designed to develop coping skills for the future. Students enter the World of Exegesis through a time warp and meet Hetero-Friday, the state computer. At each meeting they move 50 years into the future coping with a fast-changing culture while learning methods used by futurists. The book presents step-by-step lessons for 11 hours of class instruction; 18 task cards; 9 learning centers with 20 multi-disciplinary activities; background information on future problems, trends, systems, and forecasting techniques; and a list of resources, community experts, books, and films.
Target *Audience:*	Grades 5 through 9
Materials *Provided:*	This 8½ × 11" book of 287 pages includes all the information and lessons necessary to teach this simulation in futuristics. Some of the learning centers are more meaningful when readily available science fiction stories are borrowed from the library for student reading. The Task Card Packet #1 contains the 18 activities which identify trends and systems. These oaktag cards can be used by small groups or added to an already existing unit. The Student/Teacher Packet #2 contains the materials from the book which are copied for student distribution. The Individual Student Learning Centers Packet #4 includes all 15 learning centers on 5 × 8¼ oaktag. These

activities can be used by a small group or added to an existing unit.

Teacher's Guide: This guide is a detailed study of futuristics. The teacher is given an organized sequence of lessons to develop key issues and personal time lines, improve communicative and planning abilities, identify systems and trends, and complete cross-impact matrices, future wheels, and Delphi matrices. The students also participate in a Year 2000 Creative Problem-Solving simulation.

Subject Matter and Teaching Strategy: This unit is a part of the Independent Study Process (I.S.P.). The I.S.P. has three phases: Teacher-Led, Independent Study, and Seminar. In the teacher-led phase, the teacher introduces the depth and breadth of an academic area. Then the student picks a topic that interests him/her and completes an independent study. The seminar teaches complicated skills such as computer programming, photography, and the Creative Problem-Solving Process. This guide is one of the teacher-led units. It is particularly appropriate for gifted students with mature work-study skills. It can be used with gifted students in a regular classroom or in a resource room. Learning centers and task cards can be used with small groups.

Rationale: This guide is based upon the curriculum principles of Taba. Students are taught an organized structure of knowledge and skills to promote retention and transfer. The theories of Renzulli and the creative and cognitive skills of Williams, Bloom, Taylor, and Parnes are incorporated in this cohesive curriculum unit.

What:	*Imagination Express: Saturday Subway Ride*
	Gary A. Davis and Gerald DiPego

Published By:	DOK Publishers, Inc.
	P.O. Box 605
	East Aurora, NY 14052

How To Order:	Order from publisher.
	List price: $5.95
	Consumable items: Detachable master maker sheets to be used with spirit masters or mimeo stencils.

Description:	The *Imagination Express: Saturday Subway Ride* is an imaginative 66 page workbook and a travel story-exercise format designed to teach creative-thinking techniques and positive attitudes toward creativity. Pupils buy a ticket for the Imagination Express by paying with a song or story or whatever other imaginative thing each can create and then it is "All Aboard" for a wild, fun-filled adventure which takes them from Kansas City to Pittsburg to Dublin to Tokyo to Santa Monica and back. Just like Alice in Wonderland, the pupil will meet strange and wonderful people and places, experience the fun of creating fantastic happenings and solve interesting problems in the *Saturday Subway Ride*.

Target Audience:	The workbook was specifically designed to be used over a two-to-four month period with intermediate (3–8) grade level pupils.

Materials Provided:	One story booklet. This booklet contains seven stories based upon an imaginative subway ride from Kansas to Dublin and back again.
	Eighteen master sheets. These detachable sheets provide exercises in flexible, fluent and elaborative thinking which are used in conjunction with the story booklet.

Teacher's Guide:	*Imagination Express* is intended to be a "point of departure" for elementary grade teachers to begin a new kind of thinking about instructional planning and materials. *Imagination Express* is a valuable resource of ideas for the enthusiastic teacher in fostering creativity in students.

Subject
Matter
and Teaching
Strategy:

Imagination Express provides practice in verbal expression and in creative writing. The story theme is an around-the-world subway ride with fantastic episodes at each stop, some of which are supplied by the pupil.

Throughout the course of the journey, the pupil is encouraged to demonstrate his understanding of five creative problem-solving techniques by means of the pertinent workbook exercises presented throughout the text. The student learns to identify important attributes or parts of an object, considering each attribute as a source of potential improvement. Students consider each item on a prepared list as a possible source of innovation with respect to a given problem. By means of a metaphorical activity, students are asked to consider how other people, animals, and plants solve a similar problem. Groups of students use the "brainstorming" technique to find solutions for problems such as "how to turn a classroom into a foreign planet."

The practice activities given in the workbook should help pupils develop verbal fluency and imaginative writing skills.

Rationale:

The *Imagination Express: Saturday Subway Ride* was intended to stimulate the creative problem-solving ability of pupils by fostering a favorable predisposition toward "wild" or imaginative ideas. It is possible to learn to be a more productive and more original thinker by focusing upon the development of strategies of thinking which facilitate the generation of ideas. A child's creative ability can be improved through practice with the techniques of generating new ideas.

The creative development of children depends largely upon the sensitivity and imagination of teachers and curriculum developers. *Imagination Express* encourages the teacher to find new and different experiences for children.

What:	*Joust for Fun* Edith J. S. Doherty and Louise C. Evans
Published By:	Synergetics P.O. Box 84 East Windsor Hill, CT 06028
How To Order:	Order from publisher List Price: $22.95 (Teacher's Guide)
Description:	*Joust for Fun* explores the culture of the Middle Ages, culminating in a Knighting Ceremony and a Medieval Banquet. Teachers are provided with step-by-step lesson plans for 13 hours of instruction; 27 learning centers with 76 multi-disciplinary activities; background information on the feudal system, Black Death, crusades, and costumes; and lists of resources, community experts, books, films, and realia.
Target Audience:	Grades 4 through 8.
Materials Provided:	This 8½″ × 11″ book of 244 pages includes all the information and lessons needed to teach this curriculum unit.
Teacher's Guide:	This guide is a detailed study of medieval culture. The teacher is given an organized sequence of lessons to introduce the roles of the serf, church, knight, king, and merchant. Students examine the Byzantine Empire, the Islamic World, Gothic and Romanesque architecture, and the medieval mind. Learning centers give students an opportunity to investigate tortures, weapons, castle design, feudal specters, tournaments, holidays, cathedral architecture, food, entertainment, guilds, and medieval literature.
Subject Matter and Teaching Strategy:	This unit is a part of the Independent Study Process (I.S.P.). The I.S.P. has three phases: Teacher-Led, Independent Study, and Seminar. In the teacher-led phase, the teacher introduces the depth and breadth of an academic area. Then the student picks a topic that interests him/her and completes an independent study. The seminar teaches complicated skills such as computer programming, photography, and the Creative Problem-Solving

Process. This guide is one of the teacher-led units. It can be used with gifted in a regular classroom, in a resource room, or as a project for two or three students. Learning centers can be used with small groups.

Rationale: This guide is based upon the curriculum principles of Taba. Students are taught an organized structure of knowledge and skills to promote retention and transfer. The theories of Renzulli and the creative and cognitive skills of Williams, Bloom, Taylor, and Parnes are incorporated in this cohesive curriculum unit.

What:	*JUST THINK PROGRAMS* to teach thinking in pre and elementary schools (8 books). Sydney Billig Tyler *STRETCH THINK PROGRAMS* for wider age bands and combination classes (3 books). Sydney Billig Tyler
Published By:	Thomas Geale Publications Inc. 1142 Manhattan Avenue, Drawer C.P. 223 Manhattan Beach, California 90266
How To Order:	Order from publisher. Free descriptive flier with order form available. 13 soft cover, reusable books (see Target Audience). Price range: $10.00 to $35.00 per book (see Target Audience) plus 5% shipping and handling. ($1.50 minimum).
Description:	JUST THINK is a series of programs to teach elementary and pre school children to think. Instead of being passive learners, handed pencils and paper, the students become active participants in the process of expanding and developing creative and cognitive skills. The programs parallel multi-curricular requirements and adapt to a wide learner range. *Just Think* can be used with equal success by parents and includes lesson worksheets, a full set of directions, and plans for a complete, sequential, school year program.
	Results of out-of-cycle legal compliance review June 24, 1983: These programs "were found to be in compliance by the review panel and, therefore, meet the social content requirements of Education Code Sections 60040–60044", State of California Department of Education.
Target Audience:	Young Think: Ages 3 & 4. May be used in Kindergarten. $15.00 Just Think 1: Kindergarten—Ages 5 & 6. $15.00 Just Think 2: Ages 6 & 7—Grades 1 or 2. $25.00 Just Think 3: Ages 7 & 8—Grades 2 or 3. $25.00 Just Think 4: Ages 8 & 9—Grades 3 or 4. $25.00 Just Think 5: Ages 9 & 10—Grades 4 or 5. $25.00 Just Think 6: Ages 10 & 11—Grades 5 or 6. $25.00 Just Think 7: Ages 11 & 12—Grades 6 or 7. $25.00 NOTE: Just Think 6 and 7 may be used quite successfully in junior high grades.

Stretch Think One: Ages 5, 6 & 7; Grades K, 1, 2. $35.00
Stretch Think Two: Ages 7, 8, 9 & 10; Grades 2, 3, 4. $35.00
Stretch Think Three: Ages 11, 12, 13, 14; Grades 5, 6, 7, 8. $35.00
Project Overview: The Subject of Thinking. $10.00 (Explains program development and background.)
Same Book: Just Think Programs. $15.00 (Gives a part of each program in the 8 book series.)
Program Matrix: Shows which other curriculum units are built into the program.

Materials Provided: Each book contains everything needed by the teacher for the year.
(See description above)

Teacher's Guide: Each book has complete instructions with the lessons and program.

Subject Matter And Teaching Strategy: For Just Think Programs, two types of lessons are given for each of the thirty week school year. In Young Think, 100 lessons are given to cover the two age groups in the pre school situation. Stretch Think Programs are based upon a 25-week year, but include extra lessons for each week.

Note: Just Think 1 has both lesson types, but fewer total lessons for a half day school year.

1. Cognitive Skill Development Lessons, in which the children learn to use and extend thinking abilities through an examination of specific issues and problems.
2. Lateral Skill Development Lessons, in which the children explore a wide range of methods and solutions to creative problems and design ideas.

Rationale: Sydney Tyler, in cooperation with Dr. Edward deBono, Director, The Cognitive Research Trust (Cambridge, England) developed these programs to provide elementary teachers and schools with a full curriculum for teaching children to think.

What:	*Learning Through Creative Thinking* and *Mathematics Through Creative Thinking* M. Ann Dirkes
Published By:	DOK Publishers, Inc. P.O. Box 605 East Aurora, NY 14052
How To Order:	Order from publisher List price: $4.95 per packet Consumable items: None
Description:	*Learning Through Creative Thinking* and *Mathematics Through Creative Thinking* are activity packets designed to develop divergent thinking and, as a result, increase student intellectual abilities and affective growth.
Target Audience:	Grades 3–6
Materials Provided:	*Learning Through Creative Thinking*—Teacher's guide, introduction and instructions for students, 70 activity cards. *Mathematics Through Creative Thinking*—Teacher's guide, introduction and instructions for students, 51 activity cards.
Teacher's Guide:	Discusses cognitive and affective objectives of the activity cards and suggests ways to implement the cards in the classroom. Activities which foster specific abilities are also presented for the teacher. Lists of possible responses to several activities may be found in the back of this booklet. These activities can be made available to students as activities are completed.
Subject Matter and Teaching Strategy:	Although *Learning Through Creative Thinking* and *Mathematics Through Creative Thinking* deal with different subject areas by means of subject specific activities, both sets of cards attempt to provide for basically the same end goals: the development of intellectual abilities, the promotion of learning in specific subject areas, and the cultivation of affective development. More specific objectives include the development of divergent production and evaluative abilities as well as problem solving techniques.

The activity cards are beneficial for use with academically and creatively gifted students in that children are aided in learning and inquiring independently.

Several factors may be varied in implementing the programs. Cards may be used with all students in the class or only the academically and/or creatively gifted. Students may do activities alone, in small groups, or in large groups (although emphasis is on independent activity). Activities may be used in a learning center, as a substitute for more routine teaching, or at home as the student has free time. Other variables include feedback, monitoring, materials use, and sequence.

Students are directed to complete activities one through five within a few days. These cards teach brainstorming techniques which are used throughout the activities. After activity #5, students may work on cards out of sequence (in *Learning Through Creative Thinking,* students are requested to work through activity #13 before working out of sequence.)

Student troubleshooters are identified by the teacher and children may turn to them if they run into difficulties. Students ask for teacher aid only if the troubleshooter is unable to help.

Rationale: School curricula are usually designed to facilitate lower level skills such as memorization of facts and concepts and understanding of concepts. Emphasis is most often on convergent production. In mathematics and in general learning, stress is placed less on problem solving and divergent responses, and more on arriving at one correct solution with little regard for the integrative processes of learning. These two programs were developed to cultivate cognitive skills and subject matter learning through the use of divergent thinking strategies which allow the child to learn continuously and on his own, utilizing high level thinking strategies.

What:	*Logic in Easy Steps*
	Anita Harnadek
Published by:	Midwest Publications
	PO Box 448 Dept. 70
	Pacific Grove, CA 93950
How to Order:	Order from publisher
	List price: $4.75 each book
	$6.95 universal teachers manual
Description:	*Logic in Easy Steps* teaches students about logic the easy way—in small, easily understandable steps, a little at a time. Each explanation includes examples and is followed by problems. Students who complete this series will have learned much of what is taught in a one-term course in symbolic logic at the college level.
Target Audience:	Books 1–3; grades 3–12
	Books 4–14; grades 4–12
Materials Provided:	Each volume focuses on a particular skill and activities are designed to focus on a specific level of difficulty. The following may be purchased individually:

Book 1 Introduction: "And" Statements

Book 2 "or" Statements Negations of "And or" Statements

Book 3 Symbols: Equivalent Statements: "And" and "or" Statements

Book 4 Review Problems for Book 1–3

Book 5 Conditionals

Book 6 Review Problems for Book 5

Book 7 More About "And" and "or" Statements and Conditionals

Book 8 Review Problems for Book 7

Book 9 Arguments: Introduction to Proofs

Book 10 Arguments to Prove Valid or Invalid—Beginnings

Book 11 Arguments to Prove Valid or Invalid—Intermediate and Advanced

Book 12 Universal Statements: Conditionals: Counterexamples

Book 13 Universal Statements (cont.): Existential Statements
Book 14 Review Problems for Books 9 and 12–13
Logic in Easy Steps Teacher's Guidebook

Subject Matter and Teaching Strategy:

The format is non-graded and thus suitable for a wide range of ages and abilities. Vocabulary and reading level in the explanations vary from about the third to sixth grade level, with a few technical terms. Difficult vocabulary in the problems is kept to a minimum while the students are learning to apply new concepts.

Rationale:

Gifted students sometimes skip steps in the logic process. As the analysis activities become more complicated, the frequency of errors increase. With the tools of logic, students are able to retrace their thinking and discover the root of judgement error.

What:	*Mind Benders* Anita Harnadek
Published by:	Midwest Publications PO Box 448 Dept. 70 Pacific Grove, CA 93950
How to Order:	Order from publisher List prices: $5.95 instruction book & solutions $4.75 each book activity $9.95 includes dittos $39.95 software A–1, A–2, A–3, Apple and TRS–80 MOD III/IV.
Description:	Activities designed to sharpen students deductive thinking skills are provided. The twelve books are supplementary nongraded, low-read, interdisciplinary, and each page has generous amounts of white space. This material can be related to Bloom's Taxonomy and Guilford's Structure of the Intellect and is validated for Mary Meeker's SOI.
Target Audience:	K–12, Warm-up MINDBENDERS K–5, "A" level (A–1, A–2, A–3) All students no matter how gifted should begin here to learn the procedure. "B" level (B–1, B–2, B–3, B–4) roughly, grades 3–12. "C" level (C–1, C–2, C–3) roughly grades 4–12.
Materials Provided:	Each volume provides students with activities designed for one level of difficulty. The following may be purchased individually. *MINDBENDERS INSTRUCTIONS AND DETAILED SOLUTIONS* *WARM-UP MINDBENDERS* *MINDBENDERS A–1 (EASY)* *MINDBENDERS A–2 (EASY)* *MINDBENDERS A–3 (EASY)* *MINDBENDERS A–4 (EASY)* *MINDBENDERS B–1 (MED)* *MINDBENDERS B–2 (MED)* *MINDBENDERS B–3 (MED)* *MINDBENDERS B–4 (MED)* *MINDBENDERS C–1 (HARD)* *MINDBENDERS C–2 (HARD)* *MINDBENDERS C–3 (HARD)*

*Subject
Matter
and
Teaching
Strategy:*

The activities provide students with a multi-disciplined approach to deductive thinking. Students are learning such skills as they actively solve deductive thinking problems and learn a systematic method for doing so.

Rationale:

The purpose of *MINDBENDERS* is to sharpen the deductive skills of students, for better reading comprehension, math, writing skills, science, test-taking skills, etc. Gifted students often possess a high degree of intuition, however, the *MINDBENDER* series teaches students a more systematic approach to problem-solving.

What	*Mind in Motion* Carolyn Powell
Published By:	Dandy Lion Publications PO Box 190 San Luis Obispo, CA 93406
How To Order:	Order from publisher List Price: $8.50 Reproducible pages included.
Description:	Creative thinking activities designed to promote divergent thinking. Questions and stimulating tasks based on everyday interests and experiences of students (e.g., advertising, photography, television, weather, etc.).
Target Audience:	Grades 3–6.
Materials Provided:	Eighty page booklet containing several activities on each page. There are 21 different topic areas, with several different activities for each topic.
Teacher's Guide:	None
Subject Matter/ Teaching Strategy:	These activities present open-ended tasks that are not directly "tied" to specific curriculum areas. Teachers can use the activities as supplementary, or relate them to a variety of basic content topics.
Rationale:	Interesting examples of activities that incorporate methods and techniques for stimulating divergent thinking.

What:	*Mission Serendipity: An Adventure in CPS*
	Audrey W. and Jan C. Lederman
Published By:	DOK Publishing Co.
	P.O. Box 605
	East Aurora, NY 14052
How To Order:	Order from Publisher.
	List Price: $11.95
Description:	This 144 page book is designed to help the reader/student learn to use metaphor and analogy as tools in creative problem solving. Students learn to see new relationships and to make unique connections between things and ideas. Combines use of creative and critical thinking skills.
Target Audience:	Teachers, grades K–12.
Materials Provided:	Extensive materials to guide teachers in planning and conducting activities; many pages can be used or adapted for students or made into slides or transparencies.
Teacher's Guide:	Book is designed for teacher use.
Subject Matter/ Teaching Strategy:	Uses a variety of strategies to promote effective "connection-making," using metaphor and analogy.
Rationale:	Draws from concepts of synectics, especially as discussed by Gordon or Gordon & Poze.

What:	*The Month-to-Month Me* Linda Schwartz
Published By:	The Learning Works P.O. Box 6187 Santa Barbara, California 93160
How To Order:	Order from publisher List price: $4.95 (add $1.50 for postage and handling) Consumable items: None
Description:	*The Month-to-Month Me* contains 40 activities which enable students to keep an ongoing journal about themselves. Exercises are divided into months, with 4 activities per month for the school year
Target Audience:	Grades 4–7
Materials Provided:	One *Month-to-Month Me* Book
Subject Matter and Teaching Strategy:	Affective learning is the main emphasis of *Month-to-Month Me*. Through the course of a school year students gain insight into themselves and their feelings by use of the activities in the book. Exercises also develop creative thinking, writing, and arts skills. Activities may be reproduced for individual students, and are well suited to independent work and use in learning centers. It is suggested that students make a book out of the activities at the end of the year.
Rationale:	By continuously working on activities throughout the school year, students gain self-awareness while constantly building self concepts. At the end of the year, children have a meaningful remembrance of themselves during the school year, reflecting their on-going emotional and creative growth.

What:	*New Directions in Creativity* Mark A,B,I,II,III, 1976 Joseph S. Renzulli, Linda Smith, Barbara Ford, Mary Jo Renzulli
Published By:	Scribner Educational Publishers A division of Macmillan, Inc. 866 Third Avenue New York, NY 10022
How To Order:	Order from publisher. List price: $44.00 Consumable items: Each book contains 48 duplicating masters of activities.
Description:	*New Directions in Creativity* is designed to develop the creative thinking skills of children through exercises in divergent thinking. The programs concentrate on improving fluency, flexibility, originality, and elaboration in the context of language arts through making up stories and sentences and working with words in a variety of ways.
Target Audience:	No rigid grade levels are prescribed, but grades K–3 for Mark A and B and grades 4–8 for Mark I, II and III are most highly recommended.

Mark A	*Grades Kindergarten–1*
Mark B	*Grades 2–3*
Mark I	*Grades 4–5*
Mark II	*Grades 5–6*
Mark III	*Grades 6–8*

Materials Provided:	Each level (Mark A,B,I,II,III) consists of a book containing a teacher's guide and 48 duplicating masters.
Teacher's Guide:	The Teacher's Guide presents a description of the history, purpose, and goals of the program. Also included is a summary of some of the theory and research that led to the formulation of the *New Directions in Creativity* series. Suggestions for the teacher on how to best use the program's activities and enhance its effects are included.

Subject Matter and Teaching Strategy:	Each activity requires a class period to complete, so the program could be used with whole classroom groups in language arts activities. The follow-up suggestions for each activity can be used to extend the material and ideas into other classroom subjects. The program could also be used effectively in an individualized or open classroom.
Rationale:	*New Directions in Creativity* has been produced in answer to a recognized need for effective, research-based curricular materials for developing children's creativity. The program is based on evidence that all children have potential for creative thought and that the exercise of their creative abilities will result in cognitive growth.

What:	*On the Nose* George G. Bear and Carolyn M. Callahan
Published By:	Creative Learning Press P.O. Box 320 Mansfield Center, CT 06250
How To Order:	Order from publisher $12.95 Includes reproducible exercises.
Description:	*On the Nose* is intended to provide supplementary enrichment activities with an emphasis on Creative thinking, problem solving, and moral reasoning.
Target Audience:	Elementary school students
Materials Provided:	Twelve cartoons, designed to provoke students to think creatively as a starting point for discussion and problem solving involving moral reasoning; exercises and teaching guidelines are included with each of the twelve cartoons.
Teacher's Guide:	A separate section of the book gives instructions for using the activities, along with suggestions for both warm-up and follow-up activities.
Subject Matter And Teaching Strategy:	The lessons are designed to provide supplementary enrichment, following Renzulli's Type-Two Enrichment, the first and second levels of Treffinger's Creative Learning model, and Stages One and Two of Feldhusen & Kolloff's Three Stage Model.
Rationale:	These exercises provide useful supplementary exercises and activities for teachers to use with students at many ability levels. They provide useful resources for getting started in the classroom in applying the models described in Chapters Two and Three of this book.

What:	*The Opportunity Discovery Process* George and Vaune Ainsworth-Land
Published By:	DOK Publishing Co. P.O. Box 605 East Aurora, NY 14052
How To Order:	Order from publisher. List Price: $6.95
Description:	A 56 page book for mature readers (Adults or mature adolescents); intended to help the reader find his/her true priority areas for problem-solving, discover effective ways to implement ideas for those opportunity areas, and put ideas into action.
Target Audience:	Adults or mature adolescents.
Materials Provided:	56 page book, with several worksheets and reproducible pages.
Teacher's Guide:	Designed as a self-instructional resource.
Subject Matter/ Teaching Strategy:	Utilizes a sophisticated "grid" or matrix approach to analyze opportunity areas and to evaluate alternatives, combined with use of creative problem solving methods.
Rationale:	A creative approach to opportunity analysis, planning, and decision-making.

What:	*Options: A Guide To Creative Decision Making*
	Dianne Draze
Published By:	Dandy Lion Publications
	PO Box 190
	San Luis Obispo, CA 93406
How To Order:	Order from publisher
	List Price: $8.50
	Reproducible pages included.
Description:	Twenty-three imaginative and stimulating lessons to help students learn to be more effective in decision-making. Includes many resources for teaching specific methods to develop alternatives and evaluate or select among options. Reproducible pages are included for each lesson.
Target Audience:	Grades 4–8.
Materials Provided:	68 page booklet, contains 23 lessons; well-designed reproducible activity pages; twelve pages of background material for teachers.
Teacher's Guide:	Instructions and suggestions included.
Subject Matter/ Teaching Strategy:	Emphasis on uses of creative thinking and higher level thinking skills in effective decision-making by students.
Rationale:	Based on a nine step approach to decision-making (defining the problem, self awareness, finding the facts, redefining the problem, looking for alternatives, predicting consequences, choosing an alternative, taking action, and evaluating).

What:	*Pioneer Skills* Edith J. S. Doherty and Louise C. Evans
Published By:	Synergetics P.O. Box 84 East Windsor Hill, CT 06028
How To Order:	Order from publisher List Price: $22.95
Description:	*Pioneer Skills* is a simulation in which students form a wagon train, face the hardships of 1840's pioneers, and learn some of their survival skills. Teachers are provided with step-by-step lesson plans for 20 hours of instruction; 10 issues of the newspaper. *The Independent Expositor,* covering historical background from 1750 to 1959; 20 projects that practice survival skills; and a list of resources, community experts, books, films, and realia.
Target Audience:	Grades 3 through 8.
Materials Provided:	This 8 1/2″ × 11″ book of 213 pages includes all the information and lessons needed to teach this curriculum unit. The skill lessons suggest homemade tools and equipment to do the projects.
Teacher's Guide:	This guide is a detailed study of the life of a pioneer. The teacher is given an organized sequence of lessons to set up the wagon train, familiarize the students with the language, tools, and environment, and simulate a trip from Independence, Missouri, to Fort Vancouver in the Oregon Territory. Suggestions are given for personalizing the newspaper and involving students in its production as the class crosses the country. The skill lessons are woven into the trip as the class faces the obstacles of trail life.
Subject Matter and Teaching Strategy:	This unit is a part of the Independent Study Process (I.S.P.). The I.S.P. has three phases: Teacher-Led, Independent Study, and Seminar. In the teacher-led phase, the teacher introduces the depth and breadth of an academic area. Then the student picks a topic that interests him/her and completes an independent study. The seminar teaches complicated skills such as computer program-

ming, photography, and the Creative Problem-Solving Process. This guide is one of the teacher-led units. It can be used with gifted in a regular classroom, in a resource room, or as a project for two or three students.

Rationale: This guide is based upon the curriculum principles of Taba. Students are taught an organized structure of knowledge and skills to promote retention and transfer. The theories of Renzulli and the creative and cognitive skills of Williams, Bloom, Taylor, and Parnes are incorporated in this cohesive curriculum unit.

What:	*Primary Independent Study* by Edith J. S. Doherty and Louise C. Evans
Published *By:*	Synergetics P.O. Box 84 East Windsor Hill, CT 06028
How *To* *Order:*	Order from publisher List Price: $7.95 (Teacher's Guide) $7.95 (Primary Independent Study Booklet/ Packet #7, 5 student booklets) or in quantities of 5 or more Consumable Items: Primary Independent Study Booklet
Description:	*Primary Independent Study* is designed to teach the beginning reader and non-reader the skills of independent study. It presents teaching strategies that supplement *Self-Starter Kit for Independent Study,* and lesson plans for note-taking, idea production, and location of library sources. Problems of primary students are also discussed. A special 18 page booklet, Primary Independent Study Booklet, has been created for beginning readers that describes each step in simple vocabulary and allows space for students' responses.
Target *Audience:*	Grades K through 3.
Materials *Provided:*	The 7½ × 11″ book of 68 pages provides a reduced copy of the Primary Independent Study Booklet. The 8½ × 11″ Primary Independent Study Booklets are available in groups of 5 as Packet #7.
Teacher's *Guide:*	This guide restricts itself to discussing those guidelines peculiar to primary students. *Self-Starter Kit for Independent Study* is needed to understand the complete Independent Study Process.
Teacher *Strategy* *and* *Subject* *Matter:*	This book has been used in a gifted resource room and in a regular classroom. It is meant to follow a teacher-led unit on some area of study, but may be used to teach independent study to gifted students with already identified interests.

Rationale: This manual is based upon the curriculum principles of Taba, the theories of Renzulli, and the creative and cognitive skills as described by Bloom, Williams, Taylor, and Parnes.

What:	*The Purdue Creative Thinking Program*
Published By:	Gifted Education Resource Institute Purdue University West Lafayette, Indiana
How To Order:	John F. Feldhusen, Gifted Education Resource Institute, Education Department Purdue University, West Lafayette, Indiana 47907 List price: $155 For: Thirty-four taped programs and one set of 3–4 exercises per program. Consumable items: Exercise worksheets.
Description:	*The Purdue Creative Thinking Program* consists of 34 audiotaped programs and a set of three or four printed exercises for each program. The taped program consists of two parts: a three- to four-minute presentation designed to teach a principle or idea for improving creative thinking, and an eight- to ten-minute story about a famous American pioneer. The exercises for each programs consist of printed directions, problems, or questions which are designed to provide practice in originality, flexibility, fluency, and elaboration in thinking.
Target Audience:	Grade levels 4, 5, and 6.
Materials Provided:	Cassette tapes. 34 programs on 8 tapes, each 15 minutes long, giving specific suggestions for creative thinking and an historical story narrated by a professional radio announcer and dramatized with sound effects and background music. The program closes with an introduction to the first creativity exercise.
Exercise Worksheets:	A series of three or four creativity exercises accompanies each tape. The exercises are to be duplicated on 8½″ × 11″ paper and distributed to students. One set of exercises for each tape is provided with the initial order.
Teacher's Guide:	A teacher's manual accompanies the program. It gives a brief description and rationale of the program. Written transcripts of the audiotapes are presented along with a statement of the required exercises. General guidelines for

the teacher are also provided for help in using the series, along with a set of specific directions for proper administration of the program.

Subject Matter and Teaching Strategy: The content of the audiotapes focuses on social studies. The series also teaches skills (writing and listening) which are relevant to the language arts.

The program is designed to be administered in a group setting. However, it can be easily adapted to an individualized learning center activity.

Rationale: The program is designed to develop student's divergent thinking skills. Specifically, the exercises provide training in fluent, flexible, original, and elaborative thinking. These thinking skills increase a child's creative thinking and problem-solving ability.

What:	*Scamper On* by Bob Eberle
Published By:	DOK Publishers P.O. Box 605 East Aurora, NY 14052
How To Order:	Order from publisher $5.95 Reuseable
Description:	This book reviews the use of Osborn's idea-spurring questions in checklist form, to promote imagination development. Using games that call for the use of visualization and imagery, participants can develop new and varied ideas. Ten new games are included, which build upon the author's earlier publication (*Scamper*).
Target Audience:	Elementary students; the book also contains a section on using Scamper with adults.
Materials Provided:	The book includes instructions, illustrations, and complete text to enable you to use the 10 imagination games with a group.
Teacher's Guide:	The first ten pages of the book provide sufficient information to enable the teacher to use the games successfully.
Subject Matter and Teaching Strategy:	The imagination games use familiar but unusual content that is not directly related to any specific curriculum area; the major emphasis is to use *games* to promote imagination development and creative expression.
Rationale:	In Appendix I, the author illustrates the relationship of the *Scamper On* games and strategies to Frank Williams' model, and in Appendix IV to the Guilford *Structure of Intellect* model.

What:	*Secrets and Surprises*
	Joe Wayman and Lorraine Plum
Published By:	Good Apple, Inc.
	Box 299
	Carthage, Illinois 62321
How To Order:	Order from publisher
	List price: $7.95
	Consumable items: None

Description: *Secrets and Surprises* consists of eighteen units each divided into three parts: Motivation, Move and Imagine, and Related Activities. The units are designed to develop language skills, imagination, concentration, sensory awareness, self-concept, social interaction, spontaneity and psychomotor skills.

Target Audience: Grades K–8

Materials Provided: One *Secrets and Suprises* book

Subject Matter and Teaching Stragegy: Each unit begins with a motivation goal, a short activity or reading which the teacher presents to the class. This is followed by a move and imagine activity aimed at building creative thinking skills, psychomotor abilities, self-concept, and sensitivity to oneself, others and the use of space. Each unit concludes with several related activities, including brainstorming and individual and group projects, which aid writing, speaking, listening, creativity and other skills.

Rationale: Children's energy can be used to facilitate learning if the teacher incorporates movement and imagination into the regular classroom learning. Language development should include not only intellectual processes, but also emotional and physical aspects of development. This book provides the structure and stimuli for children to create their own experiences, thus developing language not from words, but from images and experiences.

What:	*Self-Starter Kit for Independent Study* by Edith J. S. Doherty and Louise C. Evans
Published *By:*	Synergetics P.O. Box 84 East Windsor Hill, CT 06028
How *To* *Order:*	Order from publisher List Price: $18.00 (Teacher's Guide) $5.00 (Independent Study Record Folder Packet #8, 10 folders) Consumable Items: Independent Study Record Folder
Description:	*Self-Starter Kit for Independent Study* is designed to teach intermediate and junior high students the skills of research and thinking through the Independent Study Process (I.S.P.). The I.S.P. has three phases: Teacher-Led, Independent Study, and Seminar. In the teacher-led phase the teacher introduces the depth and breadth of an academic area. Then the student picks a topic that interests him/her and completes an independent study. The seminar teaches complicated skills such as computer programming, photography, and the Creative Problem-Solving Process. This manual explains how to teach independent study. Independent study is divided into nine steps: (1) Selection of a Topic: (2) Making A Schedule; (3) Writing First Objectives: (4) Finding the Resources; (5) Recording Ideas—the Notes; (6) Writing the Final Objectives; (7) Student-Teacher Conference; (8) Making the Product; and (9) Evaluation Processes plus recording procedures. While conducting research, students are introduced to Bloom's Taxonomy of Cognitive Objectives. They then use the taxonomy to formulate questions whose answers show the depth of their research and the extent of their efforts to create new ideas.
Target *Audience:*	Grades 3 through 8
Materials *Provided:*	The 8½ × 11″ book of 161 pages gives all the teacher-made materials needed to teach independent study. It includes "Level Devil Cards" and "Concentration Cards". The Independent Study Record Folder collects all the students' materials for easy filing. There are 10 included in Packet #8.

Teacher's Guide:	This guide has detailed lesson plans for each step of independent study, ideas for products, and games to teach higher levels of thinking, interviewing, and library skills. It also discusses problems such as students who want to change their topic, those who lose research notes, and students who have poor work-study skills.
Subject Matter and Teacher Strategy:	This book has been used in a gifted resource room and in a regular classroom. It is meant to follow a teacher-led unit on some area of study, but may be used to teach independent study to gifted students with already identified interests.
Rationale:	This manual is based upon the curriculum principles of Taba, the theories of Renzulli, and the creative and cognitive skills as described by Bloom, Williams, Taylor and Parnes

What:	*Sharpen Your Senses*
	Linda Schwartz
Published By:	The Learning Works
	P.O. Box 6187
	Santa Barbara, CA 93160
How To Order:	Order from publisher
	List Price: $5.50 (add $1.50 postage and handling)
Description:	Each page provides a unique "story stimulator" in one of seven categories: writing warm-ups; sense of sight; sense of taste; sense of hearing; sense of touch; sense of smell; and using all of your senses.
Target Audience:	Grades 3–6.
Materials Provided:	One *Sharpen Your Senses* book with 24 duplicating masters. The book is divided into the seven sense areas for sequential use.
Subject Matter And Teaching Strategy:	*Sharpen Your Senses* brings together 24 illustrated story stimulators that may be used with the entire class or individual students to develop their creative thinking and writing skills via the seven senses.
Rationale:	Children are motivated by concepts they can imagine. This book gives the student real-life situations that they might encounter using their senses and ask them to elaborate on how they feel.

What:	*Stir Up A Story* Linda Polon and Bev Armstrong (illustrater)
Published By:	The Learning Works, Inc. P.O. Box 6187 Santa Barbara, CA 93160
How To Order:	Order from publisher List price $4.95 (add $1.50 for postage and handling)
Description:	Consumable Items: 48 reproducible pages. A sequenced set of black line pages designed to stimulate creative writing. The book includes activities such as: story starters; imagination boosters; mystery story writing; fable writing.
Target Audience:	Intermediate Elementary or Grades 4–6.
Materials Provided:	One *Stir Up A Story* Book
Subject Matter And Teaching Strategy:	The book is designed to develop creative writing abilities using varied activities. For example, one page gives a brief history of fables, and then the student is given suggestions for writing their own fable.

What:	*Stones and Bones* Edith J. S. Doherty and Louise C. Evans
Published By:	Synergetics P.O. Box 84 East Windsor Hill, CT 06028
How To Order:	Order from publisher List Price: $18.00 (Teacher's Guide) $5.00 (Student/Teacher Packet #3) $7.95 (Individual Student Learning Centers Packet #5)
Description:	*Stones and Bones* uses the subject matter of archaeology to introduce gifted students to cognitive and creative thinking skills, independent study, interviewing and library skills, and teaching styles used for the gifted. It also presents the following concepts: (1) components of culture; (2) development of inferences about artifacts; and (3) methods used in excavation, concluding with simulated dig and an earthen or attic dig. Teachers are provided with step-by-step lesson plans for 33 hours of instruction; 15 learning centers with 25 multi-disciplinary activities; background information on components of culture, Stone Age man, and 11 ancient civilizations; instructions for building an archaeological screen; and lists of resources, community experts, books, films, and realia.
Target Audience:	Grades 3 through 8.
Materials Provided:	This 8 1/2" × 11" book of 225 pages includes all the information and lessons needed to teach this curriculum unit. The Student-Teacher Packet #3 contains the materials in the book which are copied for student distribution. The Individual Student-Learning Center Packet #5 includes all 15 learning centers on 5" × 8" oaktag. These activities may be used by a small group or added to an existing unit.
Teacher's Guide:	This guide is a detailed study of the field of archaeology. The teacher is given an organized sequence of lessons to introduce the aspects of an archaeologist's job of selecting a site, digging, preserving artifacts, and making infer-

ences about the culture. The detailed lessons and activities provide many choices for students, the essential one, being the selection of a topic for an independent investigation. The teacher is provided with examples of issue-oriented topics as well as a list of products.

Subject Matter And Teaching Strategy:

This unit is a part of the Independent Study Process (I.S.P.). The I.S.P. has three phases: Teacher-Led, Independent Study, and Seminar. In the teacher-led phase, the teacher introduces the depth and breadth of an academic area. Then the student picks a topic that interests him/her and completes an independent study. The seminar teaches complicated skills such as computer programming, photography, and the Creative Problem-Solving Process. This guide is one of the teacher-led units. It is particularly appropriate for newly identified gifted students. It can be used with gifted in a regular classroom, in a resource room, or as a project for two or three students. Learning centers can be used with small groups.

Rationale:

This guide is based upon the curriculum principles of Taba. Students are taught an organized structure of knowledge and skills to promote retention and transfer. The theories of Renzulli and the creative and cognitive skills of Williams, Bloom, Taylor, and Parnes are incorporated in this cohesive curriculum unit.

What:	*Sunflowering*
	Bob Stanish

Published	Good Apple, Inc.
By:	Box 299
	Cathage, Illinois 62321

How	Order from publisher
To	List price: $7.95
Order.	Consumable items: None

Description: *Sunflowering* activities deal with four basic conditions to encourage imagination development, creative expression and sensitivity: imagery analogy strategies, object-to-object analogy strategies, person-to-object analogy strategies, and transforming strategies. The book describes unusual activities which combine cognitive and affective development tasks, following the author's premise that "knowledge, if it's going to be effectively learned and applied, has to be integrated into who we are, and into how we view and live life." (p. 6).

Target Grades 1–8.
Audience:

Materials One *Sunflowering* book.
Provided:

Teacher's A thorough introduction explains the author's purpose as
Guide: well as suggesting strategies for use of the book.

Subject No specific subject matter is stressed. *Sunflowering* pro-
Matter vides higher thinking experiences, seeing imagination and
and creative expression as processes of absorbing and applying
Teaching knowledge. Sensitivity development is also encouraged
Strategy: because this area has such tremendous influence on other cognitive processes. *Sunflowering* techniques are designed to go beyond traditional learning of information and to facilitate application of thinking processes.

Teachers are asked to accept all student responses in order to promote imagination and creative expression in an accepting atmosphere. Questions posed should be open-ended, and the teacher should pause frequently after questions or in discussions to allow students time for visualizing and feeling. Grading is strongly discouraged.

The book contains no chapters and teachers may follow activities through from start to finish or skip around, using the "strategy mapping chart" for optimal distribution of activities.

Rationale: *Sunflowering* looks at everything in the universe as being interrelated. Life is viewed as a metaphor, and the discovery of unique and interesting associations between images, objects and persons is therefore basic to the development of imagination, creativity and sensitivity. The growth of these thinking and feeling processes is of the utmost importance for today's students to meet future needs in an intelligent, sensitive, and human fashion.

What:	*Super Think* Hilarie Davis
Published By:	Dandy Lion Publishers PO Box 190 San Luis Obispo, CA 93406
How To Order:	Order from publisher $8.50 Reproducible pages included.
Description:	Teacher ideas for materials and activities, with examples on reproducible pages, to help students learn to question and think for themselves; emphasis on techniques for creative and higher-level questioning.
Target Audience:	Grades 4–8
Materials Provided:	An 86 page booklet describing teacher background and preparation, process discussion, references, step-by-step lesson illustration, and resources for students to use to learn to answer questions and develop their own questions.
Teacher's Guide:	Integrated into the text, along with suggested activities and reproducible pages.
Subject Matter/ Teaching Strategy:	To help teachers learn to ask questions that challenge students to think at many levels, especially levels more complex than recall or recognition of knowledge, and to help students learn to develop their own questions.
Rationale:	Emphasizes the important role of effective questioning strategies and techniques in complex thinking skills.

What:	*Thinklab* and *Thinklab 2* K. J. Weber
Published *By:*	Science Research Associates (Canada) Ltd. Toronto, Canada
How *To* *Order:*	Order from publisher Science Research Associates, Inc. Customer Services Department 155 N. Wacker Drive Chicago, Illinois 60606 List price: Thinklab $130.00, complete kit; Thinklab 2 $150.00, complete kit. Consumable items: None
Description:	*Thinklab* kits have been developed to stimulate cognitive development, especially insight, reflection, and creativity. The kits are also designed to be motivating reading programs. Cards are arranged according to type of cognitive problem and difficulty level, and are especially helpful in motivating the bright academic student to think about creative and logical problem-solving activities.
Target *Audience:*	Grade 3—Adult (*Thinklab*) Grade 5—Adult (*Thinklab 2*)
Materials *Provided:*	*Thinklabs* are stored in sturdy and colorful plastic boxes. Thinklab includes 500 cards (4 copies of 125 different cards) and Thinklab 2 contains 700 cards (4 copies of 145 cards and 8 copies of 15 cards). Kits also come with manipulative materials, student progress cards, and a Teacher's Guide. Cards are color-coded for easy identification of type of problem.
Teacher's *Guide:*	Elaborate information is given concerning the program, its purposes and its objectives. Research evidence is cited which supports the effectiveness of the program. Possible solutions to the problems are also given in the guide.
Subject *Matter* *and* *Teaching* *Strategy:*	*Thinklab* includes five basic types of problems: object manipulation, perception, creative insight, perceiving image patterns, and logical analysis. *Thinklab 2* contains six different kinds of problems. Object manipulation, creative insight, logical analysis, quantitative thinking, brain-

162

storming, and just for fun. Abilities challenged come from the middle and upper levels of Bloom's taxonomy, and problems are framed in non-academic terms to retain high motivation.

It is suggested that students begin with the lower numbered problems and work through consecutively, although it is possible to skip around according to type of problem. Students record their own achievement on student progress cards.

Because many of the problems require creative thinking, it is important for the teacher to accept more than one correct answer.

Rationale: This program is challenging for any student in the areas of creative and logical problem solving. Although it is beneficial for the unmotivated student, it is also extremely stimulating and challenging to the gifted student, because of the wide variety of difficulty levels included. An important use is with the gifted child who is bored or apathetic, as the problems are motivating and extend beyond common curricular areas.

What:	*Think Big*
	Martha Symonds

Published By:	The Learning Works
	P.O. Box 6187
	Santa Barbara, California 93160

How To Order:	Order from Publisher
	List price: $6.95 (add $1.50 postage and handling)

Description: The book skillfully incorporates Bloom's taxonomy in each lesson. The reproducible sheets are primarily creative writing stimulators which deal with the higher level cognitive skills such as synthesizing and inferring; analyzing, comprehending, and more.

Target Audience: Grades 3–6

Materials Provided: *Think Big* contains 76 reproducible pages for easy classroom use.

Subject Matter And Teaching Strategy: *Think Big* provides interesting mind stimulators for the children to work on individually or as a group. Each section deals with one level of Bloom's taxonomy. In evaluating students' work, teachers may wish to look for the following evidence of growth in cognitive skills:

1. Ability to predict outcomes imaginatively and logically.
2. Ability to identify relevant material and to ask relevant questions.
3. Ability to evaluate situations, and to present arguments and well-reasoned points of view.

Rationale: The higher level cognitive skills may best be learned by students' participation in the activities found in *Think Big*. These learning activities help encourage creativity and original ideas through independent, individual learning.

What:	*Thinking Skills That Last* Arlis Swartzendruber
Published By:	DOK Publishing Co. P.O Box 605 East Aurora, NY 14052
How To Order:	Order from publisher. List price: $7.95
Description:	Sixty-six specific, open-ended activities to challenge students' higher level thinking abilities on a variety of topics.
Target Audience:	Teachers, Grades 7–12.
Materials Provided:	Booklet contains lesson and activity suggestions, with objectives, activities, materials needed, and extension suggestions (for long-range follow-up projects) for 66 topics. Topics are classified according to several interest or talent areas.
Teacher's Guide:	Book is designed to guide teachers in developing activities for use with students.
Subject Matter/ Teaching Strategy:	A variety of strategies are suggested, using creative thinking and critical thinking methods and techniques.
Rationale:	Based on Bloom's Taxonomy and Renzulli's Enrichment Triad Model.

What:	*Will You Help Me Create the Future Today?* John R. Eggers
Published by:	DOK Publishers, Inc. P.O. Box 605 East Aurora, NY 14052
How To Order:	Order from publisher List price: $10.95
Description:	The book provides 51 classroom activities dealing with the future to help students imagine solutions to futuristic problems. The first half of the book offers a rationale and teacher's guide to futuristic studies; the second half contains the activities which may be duplicated for individual use.
Target Audience:	Middle elementary through high school. A quick review will indicate which activities are more suitable to primary students, intermediate or elementary students.
Materials Provided:	One *Will you Help Me Create the Future Today?* book. In the second half of the book, there are "Teacher Action Pages" and also "Student Activity Pages" that describe in detail 45 activities that can be used to futurize a classroom. The activities are reproducible.
Subject Matter and Teaching Strategy:	The book is designed for individual and group work doing futuristic process activities. Some "Exciting Encounters of a How to Kind" include: Headlines: 2011, My Strengths: Today and Tomorrow, and Alien Encounter. The activities require minimum preparation and each activity is accompanied by detailed teacher instructions.
Rationale:	By giving students more opportunities to become more aware of the future, students will be more capable of dealing with our fast changing world.

What:	*Wondering: Invitations to think about the future for Primary Grades.* R. E. Myers and E. P. Torrance
Published By:	Creative Learning Press P.O. Box 320 Mansfield Center, CT 06250
How To Order:	Order from publisher $12.95 Includes reproducible activity pages.
Description:	This book contains 22 brief exercises to encourage primary level students to use imaginative, creative thinking about what children and the world will be like in the future.
Target Audience:	Primary grades
Materials Provided:	The booklet includes 22 exercises with reproducible student worksheets and teacher guidelines.
Teacher's Guide:	There are suggestions for the teacher regarding preparing for the units, presenting them, and following up on them.
Subject Matter And Teaching Strategy:	There are a wide range of future-oriented topics, which include many unusual and fascinating hypothetical situations. Each one invites students to have a little fun (e.g., "what might happen if adults were banned at the movies") but also to think creatively about important present-day and future issues (e.g., "what if there were no more birds in our world?")
Rationale:	The units are designed to help teachers guide students in creative thinking *and* in thinking about the future.

SOME RECOMMENDED BOOKS ON GIFTED EDUCATION AND ON TEACHING CREATIVE THINKING AND PROBLEM SOLVING

ACADEMIC PRECOCITY (1983)

Camilla P. Benbow and Julian C. Stanley
List price: $22.50, hard cover
$7.50, paperback
How to order: Johns Hopkins University Press
701 West 40th Street, Suite 275
Baltimore, Maryland 21211

This is a collection of papers presented in a symposium at Johns Hopkins University. There was extensive discussion of the papers at the symposium which probably led to refinement and revision of papers before publication. Most of the papers deal with some aspect of the acceleration of precocious youth. Camilla Benbow reported on a five-year longitudinal study of mathematically talented youth (many of whom had been accelerated in school), the late Halbert Robinson described the rationale for radical acceleration of precocious youth at the University of Washington and Johns Hopkins University, Lynn Daggett Pollins presented research on the social and emotional development of gifted students, and John Feldhusen reviewed programs for the enrichment and acceleration of gifted youth at Purdue University. A total of twelve chapters are presented in this book.

ADVENTURES IN CREATIVE THINKING (1982)

Judith Ricca and Donald J. Treffinger
List Price: $5.95
How to order: DOK Publishers
P.O. Box 605
East Aurora, New York 14052

This book is a collection of many techniques and activities that can be used to stimulate creative thinking. Although these activities can all be used by teachers in a classroom setting, the book's principal emphasis is upon easy-to-use techniques that parents can use in their own family setting. Creative thinking can be used in a variety of aspects of the lives of children and adults. This book points the way to creative applications of creativity in our daily lives.

CHARACTERISTICS AND IDENTIFICATION OF GIFTED AND TALENTED STUDENTS, Second Edition (1983)

Frederick B. Tuttle Jr. and Laurence A. Becker
List Price: $8.95
How to order: National Education Association
1201 16th Street North West
Washington, D.C. 20036

This book presents information about the characteristics of gifted and talented youth, guidelines for their identification, and a wealth of illustrative instruments which can be used or adapted for use in gifted programs. There are also activities designed to help teachers understand giftedness and their own attitudes related to gifted and talented students.

CREATIVE LEARNING AND TEACHING (1970)

E. Paul Torrance and R. E. Myers
List price: $10.95
How to order: Harper & Row, Publishers
10 East 53rd Street
New York, New York 10022

This is an exciting book about teaching creative thinking. Its message is not limited to any particular educational level nor to any particular group of people. It is especially useful to teachers, but it can be used by administrators, supervisors, curriculum specialists, and interested laymen. The book attempts to aid teachers by increasing their awareness of their own creative potentialities and by improving their skills in identifying, developing, and cultivating the creative abilities of their students.

While theoretical considerations are not neglected, the book is primarily concerned with the things the teacher can do in the classroom to foster creativity. Some examples of what the book offers to the teacher include ways in which the teacher can acquire skills to facilitate creative learning and ways in which the teacher can understand children. Chapters are also included which are concerned with improving the teacher's ability to ask questions, foster a more creative environment, and be more creative. The book also contains sample problems and illustrations of how the material could be used in the classroom.

The authors' personal styles of writing make the book easy to read and easy to use as a source in improving teachers' and students' creative abilities.

CREATIVE PROBLEM SOLVING: THE BASIC COURSE (1985)

Scott G. Isaksen and Donald J. Treffinger
List price: $18.95
How to order: Bearly Limited
149 York Street
Buffalo, New York 14213

This book provides an extensive collection of methods and activities for learning creative problem solving. It is the first presentation of many new concepts and methods in CPS representing a major update and expansion of the original Parnes-Osborn approach. The authors have used the methods and activities with diverse professional groups and found them to be effective in teaching creative problem solving.

THE CREATIVELY GIFTED CHILD (1978)

Suggestions for Parents and Teachers
Joe Khatena
List price: $9.95 (plus $1.70 postage and handling)
How to order: Dr. Joe Khatena
8 Tally Ho Drive
Starkville, Mississippi 39759

This book emphasizes the importance of parents and teachers in recognizing and identifying creatively gifted children through testing, and then in encouraging them to develop their intellectual potential.

Dr. Khatena sees teachers and parents as catalysts for the creatively gifted child to interact with the world. The book outlines the methods of testing to identify these special children; I.Q. tests, creative thinking tests, and the like, which identify both strengths and weaknesses of the gifted child. Then the author includes exercises to encourage the child in creative thinking and problem solving. He also gives several suggestions to both teachers and parents to help support the child, reward her, reduce her anxieties, encourage her to approach learning as experimentation, so that the child becomes enthusiastic about developing her creative characteristics and making a contribution to the community in which she lives.

The book is of great value to all those who are interested in the special problems of creatively gifted children. Dr. Khatena offers sensitive insight into dealing with these children and enabling them to fully use their potential.

CREATIVE SCIENCING I AND II (1980)

Alfred DeVito and Gerald H. Krockover
List price: *Creative Sciencing I,* A Practical Approach, $7.95
           Creative Sciencing II, Ideas and Activities for Teachers and Children, $7.95
How to order: Little Brown and Company
           34 Beacon street
           Boston, Massachusetts 02106

Creative Sciencing I: A Practical Approach sets forth guidelines and specific suggestions of things teachers can do to incorporate a "creative-sciencing" approach into their present teaching style and attitudes. It details how to employ such useful strategies as interest centers, task cards, modules, and individualization . . . how to introduce "creative-sciencing" methods and techniques into virtually every subject skill or concept you present or reinforce . . . no matter whether you teach primary, intermediate, or middle school children. "Creative sciencing" as promoted in this text is more than just good science: it is good reading, language arts, social studies, mathematics, art, music, and health and physical education. It is the integration of all areas of the curriculum with the attitudes, ideals, and spirit of science.

Creative Sciencing II: Ideas and Activities for Teachers and Children is divided into three parts, Part I, "Brainstorming in Science" presents over 100 classroom activities. The activities were selected for their creativeness, student-teacher involvement, and potential content. They require little background in science, and they do not call for special or expensive equipment and supplies. Each activity is designed to present teachers with an idea, which is then expanded into a creative sciencing endeavor. Part II, "Shoestring Sciencing" is included as a reaction to the cost of science equipment and as a proof of the idea that sciencing takes more thinking and decision making than it does equipment. Part III, "Science Skills and Techniques" acquaints teachers with an explanation of the skills and techniques needed for creative sciencing.

CURRICULUM DEVELOPMENT FOR THE GIFTED (1982)

C. June Maker
List price: $29.80
How to order: Aspen Systems Corporation
               1600 Research Boulevard
               Rockville, Maryland 20850

This book is the major resource currently available to guide practice in designing curriculum for gifted and talented youth. Maker presents a general model with four major dimensions: (1) content modifications, (2) process modifications, (3) product modifications and (4) learning environment modifications. Additional chapters present a step by step plan for curriculum development, procedures for adapting the curriculum to special populations and descriptions of four programs and their related curricula. This book is an excellent resource for teachers who are working on curriculum development projects.

EDUCATING ARTISTICALLY TALENTED STUDENTS (1984)

Gilbert Clark and Enid Zimmerman
List price: $20.00
How to order: Syracuse University Press
               1600 Jamesville Avenue
               Syracuse, NY 13210

Two of the world's leaders in education of the artistically talented, both of whom have had an abundance of experience in work with artistically talented students, authored this excellent guide to the identification and development of programs for artistically talented youth. Their procedures for identification are practical, yet valid. They discuss issues related to teacher selection and preparation, how to develop curriculum and administrative strategies for program development. Overall there is a wealth of information and guidance in this book for the development of programs in an area where many schools fear to tread.

EDUCATING THE GIFTED:
ACCELERATION AND ENRICHMENT (1979)

William C. George, Sanford J. Cohn, and Julian C. Stanley
List price: Available from publisher.
How to order: Johns Hopkins University Press
     701 West 40th Street, Suite 273
     Baltimore, Maryland 21211

  This book is a product of the Ninth Annual Hyman Blumberg Symposium on Research in Early Childhood Education. It contains excellent chapters on acceleration and enrichment and comments on how the two should be fused in developing programs for gifted and talented youth. The chapter by Stephen Daurio, which reviews the research on the effects of educational acceleration, is particularly thorough and represents an excellent interpretation of the acceleration literature.

EDUCATIONAL PSYCHOLOGY OF THE GIFTED (1982)

Joe Khatena
List price: $32.45
How to order: John Wiley and Sons, Inc.
     Eastern Distribution Center
     1 Wiley Drive
     Somerset, NJ 08873

  This is a comprehensive, basic text on the psychology and education of gifted and talented youth. It provides an excellent historical background of the field of gifted education as well as an insightful discussion of types of giftedness. Reflecting the authors research expertise there is a chapter on "Creative Imagination Imagery." The book contains the usual chapters on nurturing and educational models as well as strong chapters on guidance of the gifted and special groups of gifted children.

ELEMENTARY AND SECONDARY LEVEL PROGRAMS FOR THE GIFTED AND TALENTED (1980)

Harry J. Morgan, Carolyn G. Tennant and Milton J. Gold
List price: $7.50
How to order: Teachers College Press
              Teachers College
              Columbia University
              New York, New York 10027

This book presents a framework and guidelines for developing educational programs for the gifted and talented. It provides directions for differentiating the program to the size and nature of the community. Procedures for developing curriculum according to the Tannenbaum and Renzulli models are also presented. The book is organized to provide guidance for the development of both elementary and secondary level program structures.

ENCOURAGING CREATIVE LEARNING FOR THE GIFTED AND TALENTED (1981)

Donald J. Treffinger
List Price: $7.25
How to order: Ventura County Superintendent of Schools Office
              LTI Publications
              535 East Main Street
              Ventura, CA 93009

The material in this book is in a handbook format. The book does not intend to give a complete description of teaching methods and techniques to enhance creative learning, but rather suggests practical directions for the teacher. Level I includes suggestions for these kinds of creative learning activities; brainstorming, attribute listing and forced relationship. Secondary, Level II gives ideas for teaching students the process of morphological analysis, simulations, creative problem solving and research skills. Finally, Level III provides format for these and other projects independent study, independent study project contract, and the three-stage model. The three levels presented in this book provide a format for enhancing the creative potential in every child by providing open-ended activities with no "right" answers. Creative learning can take place by working through such processes as morphological analysis, forced associations, brainstorming, and attribute listing. *Encouraging Creative Learning for the Gifted and Talented* successfully incorporates these and other processes in its three-level-format.

THE ENRICHMENT TRIAD MODEL (1977)

Joseph S. Renzulli
List price: $8.95
How to order: Creative Learning Press
                P.O. Box 320
                Mansfield Center, Connecticut
                06250

This is a guide for school personnel who are attempting to develop enrichment programs for gifted students, especially at the elementary and junior
high levels. The Triad model is well known among gifted educators and has
been used as a model for gifted programs in many schools. The model posits
three kinds of instructional activity for the gifted:

1. general exploratory
2. group training
3. individual and small group investigations of real problems

The Triad activities are developed in close relationship with the regular school
curriculum. The Appendix offers the famous "Interest-A-Lyzer" which is used
to assess student interests, skills and experiential backgrounds as a prelude
and guide for independent project activity. It also includes the "Community
Talent Miner," an instrument used to assess potential community contributors
to a gifted program. Both the Interest-A-Lyzer and Community Talent Miner
are sold in sets of 100 from the publisher.

EXPLORING BOOKS WITH GIFTED CHILDREN (1980)

Nancy Polette and Marjorie Hamlin
List price: $18.50
How to order: Libraries Unlimited
                P.O. Box 263
                Littleton, Colorado 80160

This book presents excellent guidance to teachers for the study and enjoyment of literature in gifted programs. A variety of models and approaches
for organizing reading activities within the school program are presented as
are specific units and lessons. The latter can be used in gifted classes with little
or no adaptation. The authors are also mindful of the need, in gifted programs,
to strive for the higher level thinking skills. Thus, the Bloom *Taxonomy* is
used as a guide in stating objectives and planning lessons. The book also deals

with specialized topics in literature study such as characterization, time, place, feeling, themes and values.

GIFTED AND TALENTED IN ART EDUCATION (1983)

Stanley S. Madeja (Ed)
List price: $12.50
How to order: National Art Education Association
             1916 Association Drive
             Reston, Virginia 22091

This book is a collection of chapters describing programs at the school or community level and programs at the state and national level. Notable chapters are Lee Hanson's description of programs in the Chula Vista City School District in California, Elaine Raichle's program in Irvington, New Jersey, Gilbert Clark and Enid Zimmerman's presentation of the Summer Arts Institute at Indiana University, and Clyde McGeary and Arthur Gatty's documentation of the Pennsylvania Governors School for the Arts. There are two good chapters of closing commentary by Catherine Frity on the needs of gifted youth in the arts and by Jimmy Maive and Robert Clements on followup to art programs for the gifted.

GIFTED AND TALENTED EDUCATION IN PERSPECTIVE

Joseph S. Renzulli and Elizabeth P. Stoddard
List Price: $12.25
How to order: Council for Exceptional Children
             1920 Association Drive
             Reston, Virginia 22091

This book is a collection of readings by leaders in gifted and talented education. There are four to seven readings in each of the following sections: (1) identification, (2) characteristics, (3) culturally different, (4) curriculum, (5) research, (6) successful programming, (7) model programs, and (8) an overview. There are especially good pieces by C. June Maker, Daniel P. Keating, E. Paul Torrance, Herbert Walberg, Joseph Renzulli, Robert K. Hartman, Carolyn M. Callahan, and Marvin J. Gold.

177

GIFTED CHILDREN SPEAK OUT (1984)

James R. DeLisle
List price: $14.95
How to order: Walker and Company
               720 Fifth Avenue
               New York, NY 10019

This book reports the responses of gifted children to a survey which was distributed in 37 states and territories, Canada, Germany and Australia. The children give definitions of giftedness, tell about their social interactions with peers, report on the good and bad aspects of school, and set forth their goals and ambitions. A second section of the book offers guidelines for discussions and classroom activities with gifted youth to help them understand themselves and giftedness better.

GIFTED YOUNG CHILDREN (1980)

Wendy C. Roedell, Nancy E. Jackson and Halbert B. Robinson
List price: $7.95
How to order: Teachers College Press
               Teachers College
               Columbia University
               New York, NY 10027

This book was written by members of a research team who were actively engaged in the study of gifted young children. The major focus is on preschool children, but the authors suggest that the ideas can be extrapolated to children in the primary grades. The goals of the book are to present information about the characteristics of these children, to suggest ways to identify them, and to provide guidelines for developing educational services and programs to meet their needs.

GROWING UP GIFTED, Second Edition (1983)

Barbara Clark
List price: $24.95
How to order: Charles E. Merril Publishing Co.
               1300 Alum Creek Drive
               Columbus, Ohio 43216

This is a basic text on the nature of giftedness and gifted education. Amply illustrated with photographs, it is a highly readable book which should be of great value to parents, teachers, psychologists and others who are interested in the gifted but are not enrolled in courses of instruction. The book is unique in its offering of a developmental sequence for the growth of the gifted child from birth through adolescence. There is also a strong focus on the teacher (or parent as teacher) and problems of teaching the gifted child. Creativity as it relates to enrichment teaching for the gifted is presented in great depth. The book concludes with a rich set of appendix resources including a section on teaching reading to the preschool gifted, a list of standarized tests used with gifted students, case study forms, and intellectually stimulating games. Overall the book is loaded with valuable information about giftedness and gifted education.

GUIDING THE GIFTED CHILD (1982)

James T. Webb, Elizabeth A. Meckstroth & Stephanie S. Tolan
List Price: $11.95
How to order: Ohio Psychology Publishing Company
5 East Long Street, Suite 610
Columbus, Ohio 43215

This book presents an excellent discussion of psychosocial/emotional problems confronting gifted and talented youth and their parents. It also presents many concepts which will be of value to teachers of the gifted and talented. The book has five sections. Chapter 1 presents a comprehensive overview of giftedness and the behaviors which characterize gifted youth. The second section, Chapters 2–12, focuses on characteristics and problems of gifted youth and how to deal with those problems. The third section is an open letter to parents and teachers of the gifted by the mother of a gifted child. Section four offers a bibliography and section five a list of organizations which offer services to the gifted. Overall, this is an excellent book for parents and teachers who must deal with the emotional aspects of gifted children and their families.

HANDBOOK OF CREATIVE LEARNING (1982)

Donald J. Treffinger, Scott G. Isaken, and R. L. Firestien
List price: $45.00
How to order: Center for Creative Learning
P.O. Box 619
Honeoye, New York 14471

This book is a looseleaf handbook that provides a variety of advanced concepts and resources on creative problem solving. It is intended for people who already have a basic knowledge of CPS and want to pursue additional study that will assist them in using it more effectively. The emphasis of the book is on models and methods for facilitation of CPS.

HELP! IN SOLVING PROBLEMS CREATIVELY AT HOME AND SCHOOL (1984)

Bob Eberle
List price: $4.50
How to order: Good Apple Press
                 P.O. Box 299
                 Carthage, Illinois 62321

This brief (76 pp.) paperback provides a concise, clearly written introduction to the basic methods and techniques for creative problem solving. It is very beneficial as a resource for introducing teachers or parents to CPS. The book provides excellent illustrations of CPS in action in a variety of settings.

LEADERSHIP EDUCATION: DEVELOPING SKILLS FOR YOUTH (1984)

William B. Richardson and John F. Feldhusen
List price: $9.95
How to order: Trillium Press
                 Box 921, Madison Square Station
                 New York, New York 10159

The eleven chapters of this book present lessons for the development of leadership skills. The major lesson topics are (1) an overview of leadership education, (2) goals of leadership education, (3) personal characteristics of leaders, (4) skills of a group leader, (5) communication skills, (6) group members' roles, (7) developing group goals, (8) planning group activities, (9) committee organization, (10) parliamentary procedures and (11) special talents and abilities. Each chapter includes simulation projects and supplementary activities. The material is designed for gifted youth in grades 6 to 11. All of the lesson material has gone through trial and evaluation and has been found to be effective in teaching leadership skills.

THE MAGIC OF YOUR MIND (1981)

Donald J. Treffinger
List price: $9.50
How to order: Bearly Limited
               149 York Street
               Buffalo, New York 14213

    This book provides an overview of the Parnes-Osborn Creative Problem Solving process. Informally written, it combines clear, concise narrative with ample opportunity for the reader to participate in activities or experiences to enhance comprehension. It is illustrated with many cartoons which provide effective but light-hearted aids for learning about the CPS process.

REACH EACH YOU TEACH
A HANDBOOK FOR TEACHERS (1979)

Donald J. Treffinger, Robert L. Hohn, & John F. Feldhusen
List price: $4.95
How to order: DOK Publishers
               P.O. Box 605
               East Aurora, NY 14052

    This book offers practical assistance to the teacher in planning individualized learning in easy to follow, step-by-step procedures. There are many illustrations and much sample material. Teaching strategies are presented for a variety of thinking processes, and teachers are shown how to set up a record keeping system for the classroom. All of the ideas presented in this book have been field tested by teachers. The book should also be of great value to curriculum planners, teacher trainers, professionals who prepare IEPs and teachers who work with gifted, creative, and talented students. A planning matrix is presented which shows the teacher how to relate specific subject matter content to different levels of thinking processes.

THE REVOLVING DOOR IDENTIFICATION MODEL (1981)

Joseph S. Renzulli, Sally M. Reis and Linda H. Smith
List price: $19.95
How to order: Creative Learning Press
               P.O. Box 320
               Mansfield Center, CT 06250

This book is the comprehensive statement and description of Renzulli's revolving door model for identification and education of gifted and talented youth. Based on Renzulli's well known three-ring conception of giftedness (abilities, task commitment and creativity), the model is noteworthy for its proposal of the talent pool (15 to 25 percent of the school population) and for the revolving of students in and out of the advanced level enrichment experiences as they display action signs of giftedness in addition to status signs. This book presents the theory, research evidence, and working details for implementation of the model in a school program. There are also an abundance of forms and guides in the appendix which can be adapted for local needs.

SCAMPER (1971)

Robert F. Eberle
List price: $3.95
How to order: DOK Publishers, Inc.
P.O. Box 605
East Aurora, NY 14052

Scamper is a booklet which presents games for the development of imagination in elementary school children.

In the introduction, the author explains the theory and rationale and gives directions for "Scampering." A single child, or a group of children, and one adult can play the *Scamper* games. The teacher presents ideas and cues verbally, and the children are free to explore their own imaginations. The games are designed to increase children's imagination skills, not to develop their skills in a specific subject area.

The theory and directions in the booklet are clearly written and easy to understand. Teachers who wish to increase imaginative abilities and creative skills in their students will find these games helpful.

STIMULATING CREATIVITY (1974, 1975)

Morris I. Stein
List price: Volume 1: 1974, $39.50.
Volume 2: 1975, $40.00.
How to Order: Promotion Department
Academic Press, Inc.
Orlando, Florida 32887–0017

These two volumes constitute a major review of research development and theory concerning creativity and problem solving. Volume 1 is subtitled "Individual Procedures" while Volume 2 is subtitled "Group Procedures." In Volume 1 the author discusses the creative process and criteria for the assessment of creativity. He goes on to deal with creativity as a personality-affective-emotional phenomenon and as a cognitive procedure. Procedures are then reviewed for developing the preparatory stage of creativity, the hypothesis formation stage, hypothesis testing, and communicating results.

In Volume 2, Stein focuses on such group procedures as brainstorming, creative problem solving, synectics, and various other programs. A research study is also presented in considerable detail in which cognitive and personality approaches to stimulating creativity were compared. The conclusion of the study is that both the cognitive and personality aspects are vital in developing creative thinking ability.

TEACHING MODELS IN EDUCATION OF THE GIFTED (1982)

C. June Maker
List Price: $30.50
How to order: Aspen Systems Corporation
            1600 Research Boulevard
            Rockville, Maryland 20850

This book provides an excellent summary of eleven basic theoretical models which can serve as guides in developing gifted programs. Each model is presented in a full or half chapter. The models include: (1) the Bloom *Taxonomy*, (2) the Krathwohl *Taxonomy*, (3) Bruner's structure of a discipline, (4) Guilford's structure of intellect, (5) Kohlberg's levels of moral development, (6) Parnes' Creative Problem solving, (7) Renzulli's enrichment triad, (8) Taba's teaching strategies, (9) Taylors multiple talents, (10) Treffinger's self-directed learning, and (11) Williams strategies for thinking and feeling. There is an excellent introductory chapter on the nature of models and a closing chapter which provides for integration of concepts from several models.

---

3 R's FOR THE GIFTED: READING, WRITING, AND RESEARCH (1982)

Nancy Polette
List price: $18.50
How to order: Libraries Unlimited
                P.O. Box 263
                Littleton, Colorado 80160

This book presents ideas for teaching reading, writing, and research to gifted students. After a basic introduction to gifted education it offers a discussion of methods of teaching thinking skills. In each of the three major sections of the book—reading, writing and research—several teaching modules are presented. These modules offer learning activities keyed to the Bloom *Taxonomy* and creative thinking. The twelve modules presented constitute an excellent teaching resource for teachers of the gifted.

TOWARD EXCELLENCE IN GIFTED EDUCATION (1985)

John Feldhusen (Ed.)
List price: $12.95
How to order: Love Publishing Company
                1777 South Bellaire Street
                Denver, Colorado
                80222

A collection of chapters setting forth a new conception of the field of gifted education. Two opening chapters by Editor John Feldhusen set forth a conception of giftedness and a conception of the field of gifted education. Chapters by Joyce VanTassel-Baska present curriculum and administrative models for gifted education. A chapter by Grayson H. Wheatley gives an overview of appropriately differentiated curriculum for the gifted, and a chapter by William Foster discusses psychosocial development in the gifted. Ken Seeley is the author of chapters on personnel for gifted education and evaluating programs. John F. Feldhusen and Leland Baska co-authored a chapter on identification and assessment in gifted education. These chapters represent a carefully integrated view of how educational programs for the gifted should be developed.

REFERENCES

Amabile, T. M. (1983). *The Social Psychology of Creativity*. New York: Springer Verlag.

Arnold, A., Arnold, C., Betts, G. T., Boyd, D., Curry, J., Fisher, J. L., Galasso, V. G., Knapp, J. K., Passow, A. H., Sato, I. S., Simon, M., & Tews, T. C. (1981). *Secondary Programs for the Gifted/Talented*. Los Angeles: Ventura County Superintendent of Schools.

Barbe, W. B. (1957). What happens to graduates of special classes for the gifted? *Ohio State University Educational Research Bulletin, 36,* 13–16.

Bent, L. G. (1969). *Grouping Of The Gifted: An Experimental Approach*. ERIC Document ED 040519 ECOO 5268.

Blackburn, J. E., & Powell, W. C. (1976). *One At a Time, All at Once*. Santa Monica, CA: Goodyear Books.

Bloom, B. S. (1956). *Taxonomy of Educational Objectives, Cognitive Domain*. New York: David McKay.

Butterfield, S. M., Kaplan, S. N., Meeker, M., Renzulli, J. S., Smith, L. H., & Treffinger, D. J. (1979). *Developing IEPs for The Gifted/Talented*. Los Angeles: Leadership Training Institute.

Callahan, C. M. (1979). *Developing Creativity In The Gifted and Talented*. Reston, Virginia: Council for Exceptional Children.

Carin, A. A. (1970). Techniques for developing discovery questioning skills. *Science and Children, 14,* 13–15.

Clark, B. (1983). *Growing Up Gifted*. Columbus, Ohio: Charles E. Merrill.

Covington, M. V., Crutchfield, L., Davies, L., & Olton, R. M. (1972). *The Productive Thinking Program*. Columbus, Ohio: Charles E. Merrill Co.

Cox, J., & Daniel, N. (1984). The pull out model. *G/C/T Magazine,* Number 34, September–October, 55–61.

Davidson, J. E., & Sternberg, R. J. (1984). The role of insight in intellectual giftedness. *Gifted Child Quarterly, 28,* 58–64.

Davis, G. R. (1981). *Creativity Is Forever*. Cross Plains, WI: Badger Press.

Davis, G. R. (1973). *Psychology of Problem Solving Theory and Practice*. New York: Basic Books.

DeVito, A., & Krockover, G. H. (1980). *Creative Sciencing*. Boston: Little, Brown.

Dirkes, A. M. (1977). Learning through creative thinking. *Gifted Child Quarterly, 21,* 526–537.

Dunn, R., & Dunn, K. (1972). *Practical Approaches to Individualizing Instruction*. W. Nyack, NY: Parker.

Dunn, R., & Dunn, K. (1975). *Educator's Self-Teaching Guide to Individualizing Instructional Programs*. W. Nyack, NY: Parker.

Dunn, R., & Dunn, D. (1978). *Teaching Students Through Their Individual Learning Style*. Reston, VA: Reston Publishing Co.

Eberle, B., & Stanish, B. (1984). *Be a Problem Solver!* Buffalo, NY: DOK.

Eberle, B., & Stanish, B. (1980). *CPS for Kids*. Buffalo, NY: DOK.

Eichberg, J. K., & Redmond, L. T. (1984). *Choosing and Charting*. Honeoye, NY: Center for Creative Learning.

Ennis, R. H. (1962). A Concept of Critical Thinking. *Harvard Educational Review. 32*, 81–111.

Evans, C. (1978). *Elementary Magnet Vanguard Plan Evaluation.* ERIC Document ED 157 908.

Feldhusen, H. (1981). Teaching gifted, creative, and talented students in an individualized classroom. *Gifted Child Quarterly, 25,* 108–111.

Feldhusen, J. F. (1983). The Purdue Creative Thinking Program. In I. S. Sato (Ed.) *Creativity Research and Educational Planning.* Los Angeles: National/State Leadership Training Institute for The Gifted and Talented, 41–46.

Feldhusen, J. F., Bahlke, S. J., & Treffinger, D. J. (1969). Teaching creative thinking. *Elementary School Journal, 70,* 48–53.

Feldhusen, J. F. (In press) The teacher of gifted students. *Gifted Education International.*

Feldhusen, J. F., & Clinkenbeard, P. R. (1982). Summer programs for the gifted: Purdue's residential programs for high achievers. *Journal for the Education of The Gifted, 5,* 178–184.

Feldhusen, J. F., Hynes, K. P., & Richardson, W. D. (1977). Curriculum materials for vocational organizations. *Clearing House, 50,* 224–226.

Feldhusen, J. F., & Kolloff, M. B. (1978). A three-stage model for gifted education. *G/C/T, 1,* 3–5 and 53–58.

Feldhusen, J. F., & Kolloff, M. B. (1979). A rationale for career education activities in the Purdue three-stage enrichment model for gifted education. *Roeper Review, 2,* 13–17.

Feldhusen, J. F., & Moore, D. L. (1979). A simplified creative problem solving model. *Journal for The Education of The Gifted, 3,* 61–72.

Feldhusen, J. F., Rand, D., & Crowe, M. (1975). Designing open and individualized instruction at the elementary level. *Educational Technology, 15,* 17–21.

Feldhusen, J. F., & Reilly, P. (1983). The Purdue secondary model for gifted education: A multi-service program. *Journal for the Education of the Gifted, 6,* 230–244.

Feldhusen, J. F., & Sokol, L. (1982). Extra-school programming to meet the needs of gifted youth. *Gifted Child Quarterly, 26,* 51–56.

Feldhusen, J. F., & Wyman-Robinson, A. J. (1980). Super Saturday: Design and implementation of Purdue's special program for gifted children. *Gifted Child Quarterly, 24,* 15–21.

Firestien, R. L., & Treffinger, D. J. (1983). Creative Problem Solving: guidelines and resources for effective facilitation. *G/C/T Magazine,* January–February, 2–10.

Flack, J. D., & Feldhusen, J. F. (1983). Future studies in the curriculum framework of the Purdue three-stage model. *G/C/T, 27,* 1–9.

Gallagher, J. J. (1975). *Teaching the Gifted Child* (2nd Ed.) Boston: Allyn and Bacon, Ch. 9.

Gallagher, J. J., Weiss, P., Oglesby, K., & Thomas, T. (1983). *The Status of Gifted/Talented Education: United States Surveys of Needs, Practices and Policies.* Los Angeles: Venture County Superintendent of Schools.

Getzels, J. W., & Dillon, J. T. (1973). The nature of giftedness and the education of the gifted. In R. M. W. Travers (Ed.) *Second Handbook of Research on Teaching.* Chicago: Rand McNally, 689–731.

Getzels, J., & Jackson, P. (1962). *Creativity and Intelligence.* New York: John Wiley.

Glaser, R. (1984). Education and thinking. *American Psychologist, 39,* 93–104.

Goertzel, M. G., Goertzel, V., & Goertzel, T. G. (1978). *300 Eminent Personalities.* San Francisco: Jossey-Bass.

Gordon, W. J. J. (1961). *Synectics.* New York: Harper & Row.

Gordon, W. J. J., & Poze, T. (1975). *Strange and Familiar.* Cambridge, MA: Porpoise Books.

Gordon, W. J. J., & Poze, T. (1980). SES synectics and gifted education today. *Gifted Child Quarterly, 24,* 147–151.

Gowan, J. C. (1978). Creativity and the gifted child movement. *Journal of Creative Behavior, 12,* 1–13.

Gross, R. (1982). *The Independent Scholar's Handbook.* Reading, MA: Addison-Wesley.

Guilford, J. P. (1967). The Nature of Human Intelligence. New York: McGraw-Hill.

Guilford, J. P., Hoepfner, R. (1971). *The Analysis of Intelligence.* New York: McGraw-Hill.

Harnadek, A. (1976). *Critical Thinking,* Book One. Pacific Grove, CA: Midwest Publications.

Harnadek, A. (1978). *Deductive Thinking Skills.* Troy, Michigan: Midwest Publications.

Harnadek, A. (1980). *Critical Thinking,* Book Two. Pacific Grove, CA: Midwest Publications.

Homeratha, L., & Treffinger, D. (1980). *Independent Study Folders.* Buffalo, NY: DOK.

Isaken, S. G. (1983). Toward a model for the facilitation of creative problem solving. *Journal of Creative Behavior, 17,* 18–31.

Isaksen, S. G., & Treffinger, D. J. (1985). *Creative Problem Solving: The Basic Course.* Buffalo, NY: Bearly Limited.

Juntune, J. (1981). *Successful Programs for the Gifted and Talented.* St. Paul: National Association for Gifted Children.

Keating, D. P. (1979). Secondary school programs. In A. H. Passow (Ed.) *The Gifted and the Talented: Their Education and Development, The Seventy-eighth yearbook of the National Society for the Study of Education.* Chicago: University of Chicago Press.

Kerr, B. A. (1981). *Career Education for the Gifted and Talented.* Columbus, Ohio: The ERIC Clearinghouse on Adult, Career and Vocational Education.

Kulik, C. C., & Kulik, J. A. (1982). Effects of ability grouping on secondary school students: A meta-analysis of evaluation findings. *American Educational Research Journal, 19,* 415–428.

Kulik, J. A., & Kulik, C. C. (1984). Effects of accelerated instruction on students. *Review of Educational Research, 54* (3), 409–425.

Maker, C. J. (1982). *Teaching Models in Gifted Education.* Rockville, MD: Aspen Systems.

Marion Community Schools (Indiana) (1978). Project UP, Guidelines for Elementary Teachers. Marion, Indiana: Marion Schools.

Martinson, R. A. (1972). Research on the gifted and talented: Its implications for education. In S. P. Marland (Ed.) *Education of the Gifted and Talented,* Volume 2. Background Papers submitted to the U.S. Office of Education. Washington, D.C.: U.S. Government Printing Office, A–1 to A–79.

Martinson, R. L. (1961). Educational Programs for The Gifted: A Report To The California Legislature. ERIC Document ED 100072.

Merrifield, P. R., Guilford, J. P., Christensen, P. R., & Frick, J. W. (1962). *The Role of Intellectual Factors* in Problem Solving. Psychological Monographs, No. 10.

Milne, B. G. (1982). *Vocational Education for Gifted and Talented Students.* Columbus, Ohio: The National Center for Research in Vocational Education.

Moore, B. A., Feldhusen, J. F., & Owings, S. (1978). *The Professional Career Exploration Program for Minority and/or Low Income Gifted and Talented High School Students.* West Lafayette, IN: Education Department, Purdue University.

Naisbitt, J. (1982). *Megatrends.* New York: Warner Books.

Noller, R. B. (1977). *Scratching the Surface of Creative Problem-Solving: A Bird's Eye View of CPS*. Buffalo: DOK.

Noller, R. B., Treffinger, D. J., & Houseman, E. D. (1979). *It's a Gas to be Gifted: CPS for the Gifted & Talented*. Buffalo: DOK.

OrRico, M. J., & Feldhusen, J. F. (1979). Career education for the gifted and talented: Some problems and solutions. *G/C/T*, Nov–Dec.

Osborn, A. (1963). *Applied Imagination*. New York: Scribners.

Parnes, S. J. (1967). *Creative Behavior Guidebook*. New York: Scribner's.

Parnes, S. J. (1977). Guiding creative action. *Gifted Child Quarterly, 21*, 460–476.

Parnes, S. J. (1981). *The Magic of Your Mind*. Buffalo, NY: Creative Education Foundation.

Parnes, S. J., Noller, R. B., & Biondi, A. M. (1977). *Guide to Creative Action*. New York: Charles Scribner.

Phillips, J. K. (1982). Foreign language education. In H. E. Mitzel (Ed.) *Encyclopedia of Educational Research*. New York: The Free Press, 702–709.

Reese, H. W., Parnes, S. J., Treffinger, D. J., & Kaltsounis, G. (1976). Effects of a creative studies program on Structure of Intellect Factors. *Journal of Educational Psychology, 68*, 401–410.

Redmond, L. T. (1984). *Pocketful of Projects*. Honeoye, NY: Center for Creative Learning.

Renzulli, J. S. (1972). *An Evaluation of Project Gifted*. ERIC Document ED 093135 88 ECO62266.

Renzulli, J. S. (1977). *The Enrichment Triad Model*. Mansfield Center, CT: Creative Learning Press.

Renzulli, J. S. (1978). What makes giftedness? Reexamining a definition. *Phi Delta Kappan, 59*, 180–184.

Renzulli, J. S. (1982). What makes a problem real: stalking the elusive meaning of qualitative differences in gifted education. *Gifted Child Quarterly, 26*, 147–156.

Renzulli, J. S. (1983). Guiding the gifted in the pursuit of Real Problems: The Transformed Role of the Teacher. *Journal of Creative Behavior, 17*, 49–59.

Renzulli, J. S. (1983). Guiding the gifted in the pursuit of real problems: the transformed role of the teacher. *Journal of Creative Behavior, 17*, 49–59.

Renzulli, J. S., & Callahan, C. M. (1973). *New Directions in Creativity*. New York: Harper & Row.

Renzulli, J. S., Reis, S., & Smith, L. (1981). *The Revolving Door Identification Model*. Mansfield Center, CT: Creative Learning Press.

Renzulli, J. S. & Smith, L. (1980). A Practical Model for Designing Individual Educational Programs (IEPs) for Gifted and Talented Students. *G/C/T*, No. 11, 3–8.

Renzulli, J. S., & Smith, L. H. (1978). Developing defensible programs for the gifted and talented. *Journal of Creative Behavior, 12*, 21–29.

Renzulli, J. S., & Smith, L. H. (1979). *Developing Individual Educational Programs (IEPs) for the Gifted and Talented*. Mansfield Center, Connecticut: Creative Learning Press.

Schreffler, R. H. (1969). A Six-Year Study of Three Groups of Students Screened for Sixth Grade Major Works Classes. *Dissertation Abstracts International, 29* A (10), 3473.

Siegel, K., & Wiseman, R. (1978). *Visual Thinking Skills for Reading and Math*. Troy, Michigan: Midwest Publications.

Starkweather, E. K. (1971). Creativity research instruments designed for use with preschool children. *Journal of Creative Behavior, 5*, 245–255.

Stein, M. I. (1974). *Stimulating Creativity, Volume 1, Individual Procedures*. New York: Academic Press.

Strain, L. B. (1970). Inquiry and social studies for disadvantaged learners. *The Social Studies, 61* (4), 147–199.

Torrance, E. P. (1962). *Guiding Creative Talent.* Englewood Cliffs, NJ: Prentice-Hall.

Torrance, E. P. (1965). *Rewarding Creative Behavior.* Englewood Cliffs, NJ: Prentice-Hall.

Torrance, E. P. (1966). *Torrance Tests of Creative Thinking.* Lexington, Mass.: Personnel Press.

Torrance, E. P. (1967). Epilogue: Creativity in American Education, 1865–1965. In Gowan, J. C., Demos, G. D., and Torrance, E. P. (eds) *Creativity; Its Educational Implications.* New York: John Wiley.

Torrance, E. P. (1972). Can we teach children to think creatively? *Journal of Creative Behavior, 6,* 111–143.

Torrance, E. P. (1979). *The Search for Satori and Creativity.* Buffalo, NY: Creative Education Foundation/Bearly Ltd.

Torrance, E. P. (1984). *Mentor Relationships.* Buffalo, NY: Bearly Limited.

Torrance, E. P., Bruch, C. B., & Torrance, J. P. (1976). Interscholastic futuristic problem-solving. *Journal of Creative Behavior, 10,* 117–125.

Torrance, E. P., & Myers, R. E. (1970). *Creative Learning and Teaching.* New York: Dodd, Mead and Co.

Treffinger, D. J. (1979). 50,000 Ways to create a gifted program. *G/C/T Magazine,* January–February, 18–19.

Treffinger, D. J. (1980). *Encouraging Creative Learning for the Gifted and Talented.* Ventura, CA: Ventura County Supt. of Schools, LTI Publications.

Treffinger, D. J. (1981). *Blending Gifted Education with the Total School Program.* Williamsville, NY: Center for Creative Learning.

Treffinger, D. J. (1982). *Encouraging Creative Learning for The Gifted and Talented.* Ventura, CA: Ventura County Schools, LTI Publications.

Treffinger, D. J. (1982a). Gifted students, regular classrooms: sixty ingredients for a better blend. *Elementary School Journal,* 82: 267–273.

Treffinger, D. J. (1982b). Editorial: demythologizing gifted education. *Gifted Child Quarterly,* 26: 3–8.

Treffinger, D. J. (1985). *Blending Gifted Education With the Total School Program.* Honeoye, NY: Center for Creative Learning (2nd Edition).

Treffinger, D. J. (1985a). *Blending Gifted Education With the Total School Program—Second Edition.* East Aurora, NY: United/DOK.

Treffinger, D. J. (1985b). Fostering effective, independent learning through individualized programming. In: Renzulli, J. S. (ed.) *Systems and models for developing programs for the gifted and talented.* Mansfield Center, CT: Creative Learning Press.

Treffinger, D. J., & Barton, B. L. (1979). Fostering independent learning. *G/C/T,* March–April.

Treffinger, D. J., Hohn, R. L., & Feldhusen, J. F. (1979). *Reach Each You Teach.* Buffalo: DOK.

Treffinger, D. J., & Huber, J. R. (1975). Designing instruction in creative problem solving. *Journal of Creative Behavior, 9,* 260–266.

Treffinger, D. J., Isaksen, S. G., & Firestien, R. L. (Eds.) (1982). *Handbook of Creative Learning.* Honeoye, NY: Center for Creative Learning.

Treffinger, D. J., Isaksen, S. G., & Firestien, R. L. (1983). Theoretical perspectives on creative learning and its facilitation: an overview. *Journal of Creative Behavior,* 17, 9–17.